MAYFLOWER

The Voyage that Changed the World

*The explorer, Henry Hudson, inspired voyagers to follow his example in
North America and Canada . . . and they did.*

MAYFLOWER

The Voyage that Changed the World

ANTHEA AND JULIA BALLAM

BOOKS

For Trudi Ballam, with love

This history of the voyage of the *Mayflower* is based on the eye-witness accounts of William Bradford and Edward Winslow, but in order to make it more immediate, we have followed the method adopted by the Greek historian Thucydides in his "History of the Peloponnesian War" (431 BC) in which he reports events, but makes up speeches such as the various characters might have spoken.

The passages from the Bible that we quote may seem unfamiliar, because we have used the text of the Geneva Bible, rather than the Authorised Version of King James, which the Separatists would have distrusted. The dates follow those used by William Bradford.

Copyright © 2003 O Books
46A West Street, Alresford, Hants SO24 9AU, U.K.
Tel: +44 (0) 1962 736880 Fax: +44 (0) 1962 736881
E-mail: office@johnhunt-publishing.com
www.0-books.net

U.S. office:
240 West 35th Street, Suite 500
New York, NY 10001
E-mail: obooks@aol.com

Text: © 2003 Anthea and Julia Ballam
The illustrations and photographs in this book have been reproduced by kind permission of the following companies: AKG London, Art Today, The British Museum/HIP, Bettmann/Corbis, Mary Evans Picture Library, Topham Fotomas and Topham Picturepoint.

Concept: Robert Dudley, Bowerdean Publishing
Design: Mousemat Design Limited, Kent, UK

ISBN 1 903816 38 6

A CIP catalogue record for this book is available from the British Library.

Printed in Dubai by Oriental Press.

Contents

GETTING TO KNOW THE PILGRIM FATHERS

Living in a world where we turn on a switch to produce light in a split second, it's difficult to imagine just how tedious it was to get a spark out of a tinderbox. In the Pilgrims' world a taper or a candle transformed the dark of night in a way that we can't begin to comprehend today, because we have light whenever we want it, along with hundreds of other conveniences that make life easy and comfortable for us. But for most people living in the seventeenth century, there was little to be done once darkness had fallen, other than to go to bed.

And living in a world where we go to the 'fridge to get something to eat, it's difficult to imagine the anxiety of not knowing whether there will be food on the table next week, or perhaps even tomorrow.

But the differences don't stop there. In our world, we don't think twice about travelling as and when we want to: we climb into a car or onto a plane or a train, sometimes for work, sometimes for pleasure. The country people of England in those days would have found such freedom unthinkable.

As a contemporary of the Pilgrim Fathers, Thomas Hobbes, put it, men lived in 'continual fear and danger of violent death', while their lives were 'solitary, poor, nasty, brutish, and short'. Life was hard and painful if you were poor, as most people were, although it was also much less crowded – there was only a fraction of the people we pass everyday in our busy cities. It's hard to imagine England as a sparsely populated country where most people scarcely ventured more than a few miles beyond their birthplace because it was too dangerous and difficult to travel. Many of the Pilgrims were born quite close to the one and only main road from England to Scotland, yet even that arterial road was little more than a muddy track, which sometimes became impassable because of flooding or massive potholes. In the Pilgrims' world, most people owned a wooden trencher and mug and perhaps a knife that would serve them for most of their lives. They knew nothing of basic hygiene. They rarely drank fresh water. In terms of understanding their environment and its hazards, both large and small, their experiences were utterly different from ours.

Their world was colder and hotter, larger and more dangerous, dirtier and much more uncertain. Many people died young – women often died in childbirth, babies often died in their first year of life. Yet despite such dangers, this brave and inspired band of adventurers risked everything in crossing from Europe to America, to start a new life in an unknown land.

What was it that gave them the courage to face death over and over again? The answer is simple. Their strength came from their unshakeable faith in God and the wisdom that comes from the Bible. The Pilgrims had a confidence in the Lord that constantly sustained them. Their convictions have sometimes been seen as extreme and fanatical, yet they enabled them to overcome enormous odds, and their faith constantly helped them to achieve the impossible, again and again.

The blue touch-paper that lit their faith was the technology of printing: the printing of the Bible as well as other religious texts enabled ordinary people in Europe to learn about Christianity for themselves and to come to their own conclusions. In this way, a generation of readers came to recognise significant similarities between themselves and the folk described in the Bible.

The Pilgrims read the stories and parables about oppressed and misunderstood people avidly, and they identified closely with the heroes and heroines of the Old and New Testaments. They understood why the tribes of Israel fled from the tyranny of the Pharaohs, since they themselves wanted to flee from the Anglican Church that forced them to worship in ways they could not accept. They loved and admired the compassion, modesty and mercy of Christ, and they wanted to see His way of praising God practised by their own church elders.

As they came to know and love the Bible, its teachings and the words of Christ, they found more and more parallels with the pure, loving and simple life they wanted to lead, and the direct way they wanted to worship. If you read the Bible without knowing anything of the Church, its archbishops and bishops, its rites and institutions amassed over two thousand years, the clarity of its message and the simple beauty of its language strike you as very direct and personal. The Bible speaks to us all in a particularly intimate way and its immediacy greatly affected and moved the Pilgrim Fathers, empowering them to achieve the seemingly impossible.

In this book you will read of the astounding courage and bravery of the Scrooby Separatists. Our account follows their lives over a period of around thirty years, years in which we must marvel at the conflicts and hardships they were prepared to confront. They were constantly harried and pestered by the forces of King James I. In their fight for religious freedom many of them died of diseases brought on by exhaustion, exposure or hunger. They were deeply afraid of the Native Americans, yet none of them suffered at their hands, and apart from one brief foray that they believed necessary for their own survival, they never engaged in any open conflict with the Wampanoags. Far from suffering at their hands, the Pilgrims would almost certainly have died, had it not been for their wisdom and kindness.

It must be admitted that the Pilgrims Fathers were not particularly enlightened when it came to their treatment of women or of other races; yet within the limited vision of their time, they showed an exceptional degree of respect for their fellow human beings. If the pioneers that followed them had shared their love of peace, humility and faith, the history of America and of the relations between settlers and Native Americans would have been very, very different.

Today you can visit Plymouth Rock where the Pilgrims landed, and see a reconstruction of the *Mayflower* and of their original plantation. You can visit England, and go to Scrooby and Boston, where it all began. You can wander through the hallowed cloisters of Cambridge University in England, and attune yourself to the serenity of Leiden University in Holland in search of the spirit of those famous leaders who made it all possible. But our world is light years away from the harsh and hungry reality of the men and women of the seventeenth century. If you want to get a real feeling of what life was like in those days, dip into this book, and read the words of the Pilgrims' own Governor, William Bradford.

Bradford's writings provide a brilliant, vivid and compassionate insight into what life was like for the Separatists. But as his account is not always easy to follow in its original form, we have taken his words and added to them details and descriptions to help you picture their experiences. We hope that we have brought the Pilgrim Fathers to life, and given some insight into the heroism of the first European families to colonise America successfully . . . the people that changed the world.

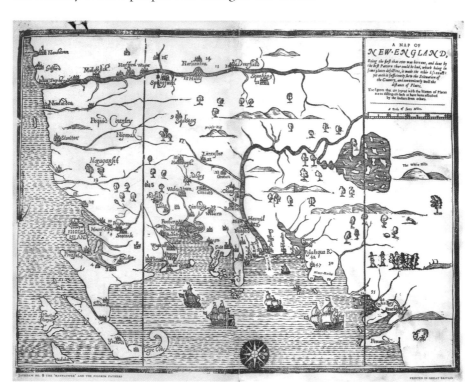

New England – the Pilgrim Fathers' destination

PART 1

Old World

Chapter

1   A TERRIBLE WINTER

The winter of 1607 was like no other. The cold was fearful. Ships were abandoned in their moorings as the sea froze around them. Large areas of the countryside became no-go areas and in England's provincial towns, the tumble-down streets of cream and black houses were draped with a spectacular array of icicles. The rivers became vast sheets of ice, and travel by road was even more difficult and hazardous than usual. Most people stayed at home and huddled around the fire until word got out that King James had decreed that the frozen Thames should be swept, and a variety of entertainments – including mazes and drinking stalls – should be set up for the amusement of the people. Visitors enjoyed all sorts of fun. There were tumblers, acrobats, and dancers on stilts; there was bear baiting and wrestlers, traders and entertainers. The air was pungent with the smell of roast pork and ox, and everywhere you looked there were side-shows and stalls festooned with flags, sweets, toys and trinkets. By day London's river was as pretty as a picture. When darkness fell and the torches were lit, it became a glittering, magical fairground.

But for some the winter was a cruel reminder of how harsh life could be in the kingdom of James 1. For the homeless, or those in prison (of whom there were many), the winter of 1607 was truly terrible. The year before, Guy Fawkes and his fellow conspirators had

King James I

been sentenced to death for attempting to blow up the House of Lords. Since then the King had become increasingly frightened of religious dissenters. Fawkes had been a Catholic, but King James was just as suspicious of other Christian groups that rebelled against the Church of England; he made it clear that anyone straying from the established faith would be punished.

This was a world where the King and his bishops decided what people ought to believe. The Church of England could be cruel and dictatorial; the King appointed clergymen to the Church and posts often went to his favourites. For some who loved and understood the lessons of the Bible and Christ, the Church seemed unfit to hold power. People of faith and religious integrity often felt that they could not support the established order – though it was one thing to hold such a belief, and another to practise it.

King James interrogating Guy Fawkes

England's worst conflicts stemmed from the power struggles of the monarchy with the Church. The country had gone through some extreme upheavals since Henry VIII had declared himself the supreme head of the Church of England in 1531. After his death in 1547, and the short rule of his sickly young son and the even shorter rule of Lady Jane Grey, Mary Tudor (King Henry's eldest daughter) had reinstated Catholicism and the power of Rome in a reign of terror that cost many Protestant lives.

When Elizabeth came to the throne in 1558 she decided to restore the Church of England. She quickly arranged a truce with the bishops who were keen to reform Bible study and education. But the next generation of bishops was greedy and opportunist – they were politicians who used their influence and authority for their own ends. By the 1580s, enthusiastic Protestants (now often called Puritans) were being cruelly prosecuted by the Church.

During Elizabeth's reign, the brave and spiritually inspired who openly challenged the power of the bishops and their Church risked losing their positions, and if they were clergymen they could even face imprisonment. So when James I came to the throne in 1603 there was a momentary ray of hope that the new king might turn out to be a more enlightened ruler and would allow greater religious freedom, perhaps even wresting power and control from the bishops . . . but it was not to be. James was anxious to build up the bishops' power, rather than to reduce it.

Committed Protestants felt that the rituals and conduct of the Church owed more to the old Catholic Church of Rome than to a proper understanding of Christ's teachings, and that they were not built on true faith but political expediency. Those that expressed this belief by setting up their own place of worship and following the principles of Christianity as they found them expressed in the Bible rather than in the rituals of the official Church became known as Separatists. Their desire to worship and pray in a self-governing religious community laid them open to persecution but they were prepared to take that risk.

The Separatists were not Puritans in the usual sense, but people of faith who felt strong enough to challenge what they saw as a corrupt order, as Jesus had challenged the corruption in the temple and the Christians of old had challenged the might of the Roman Empire. Unlike other Puritans, the Pilgrim Separatists wore colourful clothes, were cheerful of spirit and had no anxiety about eating, drinking and making merry when they thought the time was right.

A Puritan

Lincoln Cathedral – the city was home to one of many Separatist groups

They wanted a Church where priest and congregation were equal. They argued that this was what Jesus had fought for and they were prepared to do the same thing. They wanted "elders" – men of wisdom who guided the community and taught love, rather than rule by bishops through authority or fear. They were a joyous, close-knit brotherhood that loved to discuss the Bible openly. They disliked the wealth of the established Church and were familiar enough with the Bible to know that it made no mention of bishops. Despite the very real dangers, Separatist groups sprang up in Nottinghamshire, Lincolnshire and Yorkshire in defiance of the law. The King and his bishops retaliated by sending out spies to track down the Separatist rebels and stop them, by whatever means they could.

During that bitter winter of 1607, John Cooper, a young county officer who served as a guard at the Guildhall prison in Boston, found himself caught up in an infamous Separatist incident. Boston, a town on the Lincolnshire East coast, was one of the busier ports in England, and Cooper's family had lived there for three generations. Although John was only eighteen years old, he was already experienced in the business of guarding criminals of all kinds – smugglers, pickpockets, thieves and even murderers.

Scrooby – a view from the river

Just before the terrible winter set in, a large group of Separatists from Scrooby in Nottingham had converged on Boston with the intention of boarding a ship to Holland, to escape further religious persecution. The Netherlands were known to be much more tolerant than England when it came to religious matters.

The Scrooby Separatists had stayed at inns and any house that would have them, and the people of Boston soon got to know and like them. They were people of all classes; some of their leaders were educated men, but most of them were farming folk, with loving families. They were full of hope, but despite their optimism, luck was against them. It was hardly possible for them to conceal their movements, for there were a good many of them, ranging from old men with grey beards to young women with babies barely a couple of weeks old. Yet their planned escape by ship might have passed uneventfully, had it not been for the greed of the ship's captain whom the Separatists had paid in advance.

It was mid-November and several days passed before the captain sent a message to the Separatist leaders saying that the ship had been made ready, and that the men, women and children must be prepared to set sail. The group assembled in anticipation and excitement under cover of darkness, but no sooner had they boarded the vessel, than the treacherous captain gave orders to the crew to bind the hands of the travellers and lower them into the long boats. Then and there the gentle Separatists were robbed of almost everything they owned including their warm clothes, money and personal possessions. Innocent men, women and children were bodily searched and brutally manhandled.

The captain had done a deal with some of the Sheriff's officers, who joined the crew in robbing the travellers and humiliating them. Dirty, bruised, shocked and dishevelled, they were returned to land, bound and publicly disgraced. All of them, including women with babes in arms, were made to parade through the town, bearing placards proclaiming their folly and wickedness, while the people of Boston were encouraged to mock and ridicule them for their foolishness in attempting to leave the country illegally. The men were then imprisoned.

It is said that at this point, when the Separatist women realised that they were completely destitute and their husbands were powerless to protect them, that they gathered in the street in a group outside the Guildhall, where the men had been gaoled. As evening fell a number of women from the town, including John Cooper's mother, intercepted the desperate and demoralised travellers. They gave the Separatist women blankets, clothes and food to help them on their sixty-mile journey homeward, insisting that not a word would be said about the gifts, or where they came from.

As the bitter winter advanced, the plight of the Scrooby Separatists became a favourite topic of conversation for the people of Boston. During those long dark winter nights, folk would gather round the fire drinking beer and arguing about the State, the Church and those who had chosen to throw down a challenge to the bishops and the King. John Cooper's family was no exception. Although he was one of the Sheriff's men, he had not been personally involved on the occasion of the theft and public humiliation, and it was just as well. His father expressed his disgust at what had happened, and maintained that the Scrooby Separatists had been most unjustly treated. He could not bear the idea that the supposed defenders of law and order should actually rob innocent women and children, and he told John so . . . in no uncertain terms.

After a few days the Separatists were brought before the magistrates of Boston. By this time a growing number of the town's citizens were in agreement that these God-fearing folk had been cruelly mistreated. Most of the Scrooby Separatists were then set free, although their circumstances were hardly better after they had been liberated. Many had lost everything they owned, including clothes, money and belongings and that winter was colder than any known before or since.

In the end, seven of the group's leaders remained in custody in the Guildhall prison in South Street, which was how John Cooper came to meet them. He soon realised that much that was said about them was true: they were kind, gentle, and peace-loving. Every day, Cooper would lock them up, two at a time in their tiny cage-like cells, which were barely more than six foot square. Whenever he gave them water or food, they would always thank him most graciously. They seemed endlessly patient and sweet-tempered, despite being desperately cold and hungry.

Cooper made particular friends with a lively, if somewhat pale and sickly-looking boy called William Bradford, who was roughly the same age as himself. On some days John would light a brazier in the prison yard, and let a small number of the prisoners exercise. If there were a few other guards around, he would play knuckle-bones with William Bradford, and chat to his prisoner.

"So how did you come to join up with these people?" John Cooper asked with some curiosity, hoping to hear something he could repeat to his friends at the inn that night.

"I was orphaned at an early age, and brought up by my uncles in a hamlet you won't have heard of . . . a place called Austerfield. My older uncle wanted me to be a gentleman farmer, but when I heard Richard Clifton preach I realised that some things were even more important than growing

 corn and milking cows. His words filled me with so much hope and joy that I have followed him and his brotherhood ever since. He was the rector of Babworth, but the bishops deprived him of his living, accusing him of preaching blasphemy against his King and Country. Of course it wasn't

william Bradford

true, I could swear to that. Now the good folk of Scrooby are his flock and I am like one of the Israelites, only instead of following Moses I follow the wisdom of Mr Clifton and Mr Robinson who are guiding me and my brothers out of the spiritual wilderness. And although my father and mother are long dead, Mr William Brewster is now my father and his family is now my family. The Scrooby brethren are the best and kindest people in this world and will always be my greatest love (after God and Christ) until the day I die."

"Are you not afraid of falling foul of the King and his men?"

"You mean the bishops," replied Bradford in a low voice, and shivered in the cold.

"And no, I am not, for if God is in my heart, I shall always be able to walk through the Valley of Death and fear no evil, and no evil that is of man's making will ever get the better of me . . . better still, I have beaten you fairly and squarely. I think you should give me your knuckle-bones, after all this is the third game in a row that I've won. Let's hope that you're better at keeping watch on your prisoners than playing this game, otherwise you may end up with a great many empty cells, and not a single prisoner to put inside them!" said young William, laughing heartily.

"Hush, William. Do not say that, my friend. It is more than my life is worth," replied John Cooper in a low voice.

The next day William Bradford was set free, but the older prisoners remained behind bars for over a month, and William Brewster served the longest sentence.

The Sunday after Bradford's release, it was John Cooper's task to guard the prisoners while they observed the day of rest. As he descended the stone stairs to the dank prison enclosure of the Guildhall, John could hear the strong, musical voice of one of the Separatist leaders, Richard Clifton, who was preaching the word of God from a small space at the foot of the prison steps. It was bitterly cold and Clifton was swathed in a

William Brewster

blanket. A knitted cap crowned his long white hair. The Separatists were watching and listening to his every word, as were the criminals, who had never heard such an eloquent and inspired preacher before. The prisoners sat silent, gaunt and wide eyed, amazed by the spiritual force that flowed from this tall, stooping figure. Two of the guards had also entered the vault and were craning forward to hear. As Clifton drew to the end of his sermon, he

William Bradford's cottage at Austerfield (top) and (below) the cellar steps and the cellar

quoted the words of Matthew the Apostle:

> *". . . for I was anhungered and ye gave me meat; I was thirsted and ye gave*
> *me drink; I was a stranger and ye lodged me; I was naked and ye clothed me;*
> *I was sick and ye visited me; I was in prison and ye came unto me . . . "*

He commented on the text:

"There is no shame in being prisoner. The apostles and Jesus did not fear confinement. It is true that we, my brothers, are here, locked away from the world beyond, but this prison rewards us with a moment for reflection in which we may draw strength from the thoughts and deeds of Christ, who suffered Himself to be imprisoned, and is the spiritual path-finder for us all. In this deepest moment of reflection, let us have faith, knowing that the Lord will look after us, and care for us. Even more importantly, let us have faith in the love and protection He shows to our families in the world outside these prison gates.

Let us pray, brothers, and above all let us be confident of the compassion and generosity of Our Father, and the love and care He has given to our fellowship which He cherishes and safeguards . . . Let us pray."

The people of Boston never forgot the visitors who were robbed and then imprisoned in their town during that terrible winter of 1607.

The bravery and faith of the Separatists became a legend and an inspiring one, and their example seeped into the very fabric of the Boston community itself. Thirty years later, another ship set sail from that port, carrying many folk who had decided to move to the New World in order to live and work and pray in a land of religious freedom and new opportunity. Those Puritans were inspired by the courage of the Pilgrim Fathers. Among the passengers was Simon Cooper, the son of John, who had guarded them in Boston's Guildhall prison. Simon took his wife and baby son on the voyage across the Atlantic. He also took with him a box containing two gifts from his father, which he presented to William Bradford, who by then was the Governor of the Plymouth Colony. The box contained a fine leather-bound Bible and a set of knuckle bones.

Chapter

2

POSTMASTER TO MASTER DISSIDENT

If any one man should be singled out as a hero amongst the Scrooby Separatists it must be William Brewster. He was the last of the Pilgrims to be set free. The magistrates and King's spies realised at once that he was the most powerful and influential force within the group. Like two other prominent figures in the movement, Richard Clifton and John Robinson, William Brewster had gone to Cambridge University. At Peterhouse College he had studied theology, logic and rhetoric, taking the opportunity to get to know the radical scholars and preachers who were trying to reform public worship and advance the cause of religious freedom. From his time in Cambridge and afterwards, he knew many men destined to die as a result of their religious views, men whose inspired and passionate writings would become part of his own very substantial library.

THIS TABLET IS ERECTED BY THE PILGRIM SOCIETY OF PLYMOUTH, MASSACHUSETTS, UNITED STATES OF AMERICA, TO MARK THE SITE OF THE ANCIENT MANOR HOUSE, WHERE LIVED
WILLIAM BREWSTER,
FROM 1588 TO 1608, AND WHERE HE ORGANIZED THE PILGRIM CHURCH, OF WHICH HE BECAME RULING ELDER, AND WITH WHICH, IN 1608, HE REMOVED TO AMSTERDAM, IN 1609 TO LEYDEN, AND IN 1620 TO PLYMOUTH, WHERE HE DIED, APRIL 16, 1644.

He left Cambridge in 1583 and entered the service of Sir William Davison, assistant secretary of state under Walsingham. Both master and servant had many dealings with the Netherlands at the highest level. Davison soon learned that he could always depend on Brewster, and they struck up a great friendship. For a while Queen Elizabeth was delighted with Davison's diplomatic skills and the benefits gained from his negotiations with the Dutch. She praised and rewarded him generously, until the day when he became the scapegoat for the execution of Mary Queen of Scots.

Although Parliament and the Royal Council wanted to get rid of Mary after the Babington plot was revealed, Elizabeth did not want to appear to be responsible for the execution of another Queen. She indicated that she wanted Mary killed secretly. Davison protested strongly, but in the end he was held responsible for sending Elizabeth's death warrant, without having informed her beforehand – a thoroughly unfair charge. He was then stripped of his office and sent to the Tower of London, where he remained for two years, and was only released after he had paid a ruinously harsh fine.

If Brewster went with Davison to that grim place, as seems almost certain, he was no stranger to the horrors of imprisonment. The incident destroyed Davison's career. But the diplomat's dedicated assistant fared rather better. Barely a year after Davison's downfall, when William Brewster was just 23, he became Master of the Posts at Scrooby, responsible for the management of

Scrooby Manor House – home of William Brewster.

the Royal post and diplomatic communications moving between Scotland, the North and the South. Scrooby was strategically located on the Great North Road.

William Brewster's father had been the postmaster of Scrooby before him, and when the position was briefly handed over to an outsider, young William Brewster had challenged the choice of the man for the job and had been rewarded for his efforts. The new postmaster took over his father's house, Scrooby Manor House, reckoned to be one of the finest residences in the district.

Without the vision, spiritual generosity and bravery of William Brewster, it is unlikely that the Scrooby Separatists would ever have been remembered. Of all the Pilgrims, he was the one with the experience and the ability to negotiate at the highest level. Until the Boston incident he had

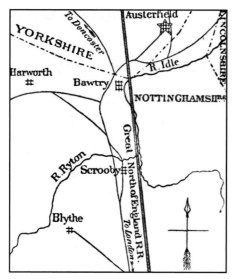

Contemporary map showing Scrooby and outlying areas

used his position to make his home a focal point and place of devotion for the rebel worshippers and for their leaders. Richard Clifton and his family, John Robinson, John Smith and many others had all sought sanctuary in Scrooby Manor House at one time or another.

Brewster's progress from civil servant to rebel can be followed through surviving records. In July 1603 his wages were increased from 20 pence a day to 2 shillings. The

last records of his salary as postmaster run from 1 April 1607 to 30 September of the same year. Barely two months later he was in prison. When he was robbed, disgraced and taken prisoner in Boston he was a man of 43. In the Boston débacle he lost more than anyone – clothes, money, possessions and a valuable collection of books were all gone forever and his comfortable existence came to an abrupt end at a stage in his life when his circumstances could have been staid and secure.

Caged up with nothing to do for days on end, he suffered terrible remorse until the news came through that his family and the rest of the Separatists had returned to Nottingham in safety. Again and again he asked God if his pride had contributed to their capture; but then, reassured by Clifton and Robinson, he accepted that no blame could be apportioned and the fight for religious freedom had to go on. After spending many hours in prayer, he emerged even more determined to take the community to a place where they could live and worship in peace. Locked away in the terrible bitter cold and darkness for days on end, he started to draw up a new escape plan. This time the Pilgrims would be more cautious, and more protective of the vulnerable members of the community – the women and children.

Back in Nottingham he was shocked to see that the circumstances of the Separatists had grown progressively worse. The lives of his brothers and their benefactors were under constant threat at all times. Houses were watched, individuals were mysteriously beaten up after dark and a profound fear and uncertainty prevailed.

A week after his release from prison, Brewster arranged, through his young protégé, William Bradford, to meet the Separatist leaders at an inn near Scrooby. The meeting place was an anteroom to the main drinking hall and only a curtain served as a screen to hide the space within. Young Bradford sat outside the temporary doorway, keeping guard in case any suspicious persons might be seen trying to overhear what was said.

William Brewster sat at the top of the table. To his right was John Robinson, the inspired and outspoken man of God, who like Richard Clifton had preached according to his inner beliefs and been deprived of his living as a pastor. To Brewster's left sat the tall, lean, bearded Clifton, the man whose voice and teachings had enraptured so many, including the young William Bradford. There were also two supporters from the Separatist Church at Gainsborough – John Wood and Edward Alden. They had ridden over 20 miles to be with their fellows in the faith.

Brewster lit five more candles, for the light in the little room was dim. John Robinson carefully hung his old cloth coat on a nail, covering the window that overlooked the courtyard of the inn and the stables beyond. The men around the long table were talking in hushed voices. When Brewster asked for their attention, they turned to face him and saw in the dancing candle-light that their leader looked very much thinner and older since his imprisonment.

"I thank you, brothers, for coming to this place this evening. Let us pray," said William Brewster and the Separatists bowed their heads in silence for several minutes.

"Thanks be to God, Amen."

"Well, brothers, we seem to find ourselves sadly deprived of the comforts of Scrooby Manor House. What is there to report?" asked Brewster.

Memorial to John Robinson in Leiden

"William White was attacked with stones when he went out to fetch some cattle for his brother," said John Robinson.

"Anne Clarke and little Mary Mason were chased on the Babworth Road by two men with ferocious dogs. Mary was badly bitten," said Edward Fuller.

"The catalogue of cruelty and injustice is long. It changes little. Have you any further plans for a flight to freedom? I know that some of our flock in Gainsborough would wish to join you in any new attempt to leave this country. We seek to join our pastor in Amsterdam where he now has a church. Whatever may have happened in Boston does not alter our view on this," observed John Wood, addressing Brewster at the top of the table.

"We must plan to leave, and leave soon. The King's men are gathering. Of this we can be sure. The Netherlands remains our only safe hope and choice, for there is still no other country that I know of where we would be free to practice our faith without persecution. The Calvinists are committed to religious freedom. They and the Government of that land will not be afraid to let us worship as we would wish and teach the scriptures in the way we would want."

"But," said Clifton, in a soft clear voice, "for the moment we must recognise that our choices are limited. We are under the eye of our enemies who would rather we had no future anywhere on this earth than find a new life elsewhere."

"We have choices, brother," replied Brewster. "Our choice is to celebrate the power of the Lord in our own way in another land, and in order to do this we must devise and follow a plan that cannot, indeed must not fail."

"Aha! It sounds as if you have used your days of incarceration with wisdom – tell us what you think we should do," said John Robinson.

Brewster proceeded to unfurl a map, setting candle sticks at the four corners of the paper.

"We must seek out and find a captain, preferably of Dutch nationality who is known as a God-fearing and worthy man by people we trust . . . and most certainly not one who would collaborate with the King's men. We must sign a contract that will allow us to board a good, seaworthy vessel at a time and day of our choosing . . . and our choosing alone. We will set out in two groups, the men in advance on horseback and foot, and the women will follow with the children, goods and chattels. This will ensure that when we leave our homes, our moment of departure will be less obvious to those that spy upon us, who I fear are growing in number every day. The men will move by road, at night, here and here," he pointed to the routes he had chosen on the chart.

"The women and children must be transported by water. I have plotted a course that I believe would be best for them to take, using the River Idle and the River Trent. This will take them eastward. Then, at a meeting point to be decided, we will rejoin our families. There are a number

The River Trent

of possible places between Hull and Grimsby that we could choose, where we might join the ship, and take passage safely to the Netherlands."

"This plan seems to be well thought out," observed John Robinson. "Have you particular times and dates in mind, and also any idea how it could be underwritten financially?"

"There are many details that must be decided, Brother John. We must search high and low for assistance in order to make it possible, but I would hope that we may proceed within the next month. Reports of the King's men and the plans they hold for us lead me to think that every day that we remain here puts our lives in danger and those of our women, children and protectors."

The Separatists agreed with Brewster. The discussion that followed weighed up the escape strategy, considered how quickly it could be carried out and who would be responsible for the various elements involved.

At the end of the meeting, John Wood of Gainsborough sat down on a stool beside William Brewster and handed him a mug of ale.

"My friend, how are you and your family? I have heard of your sufferings in prison, but I have not been able to speak to you in person these four months. How is Mistress Mary Brewster, and your new child – a daughter, I am led to believe? Am I right in thinking that she was born only days before your departure to Boston?"

"A daughter indeed, and a lovely one. The Lord has given her fair looks and a fine spirit. She smiles and laughs all day, yet her life has been nothing but turmoil and apprehension from the day she was born last November."

"And what is the name of this little one?"

"Fear," said Brewster, smiling enigmatically.

"There must be some story behind this name – I beg you to tell it to us at once and in full," declared Wood.

"Just one day before this pretty child came into the world with God's blessing, Mary and I were searching for a name, and could not decide on one. Finally, after a thousand good Christian titles had been thought of, but none preferred, I said to Mary, 'You and God will choose the name for our next child. Whether it is a son or a daughter the good Lord will provide, as ever'. But as we sat in the quiet, in the dark, beside the glowing coals of the fire, there was a sudden loud noise outside, and a rapping on the door below. And a voice cried out 'Open up! Open up in the name of the King!' My lady clung to me in terror, 'Who and what is this, William? Are we to die in our beds tonight? I am full of fear. What shall we do?' To which I replied 'We shall do nothing, Mary, but thank the Lord for giving our new child a name. He or she will be called "Fear".' And this is how my second daughter came by her name."

For the young William Bradford, sitting on guard outside the ante room the sound of merry laughter came as something of a surprise. The most boisterous laughter came from his guide and mentor, William Brewster, but then, thought Bradford, Brewster is the sort of man that would and could surprise everybody, particularly when it came to laughing openly in the face of fear.

Chapter

3   ROUGH SEAS AND GENTLE PRISONERS

D ay after day the Separatists had to make choices, as people do when they are living under any extremist regime. How long could they survive before they would be imprisoned and ultimately executed? Was it possible to worship God in their own way, living under the shadow of death? Their leaders, Clifton, Robinson and Brewster, had no doubts. Their faith was unshakeable. They were convinced that whatever came to pass, for better or worse, happened in the name of the Lord and by His will, and every twist and turn of fate was either a lesson or a gift from God. Certainly, at every turning point in the Separatists' great journey of faith, events moved in strange and unexpected ways.

By March, Brewster and the Separatist leaders were ready to set a date for their departure at the end of that month. They fully realised that, whatever they did, they risked arrest and imprisonment at any time. What they overlooked was the unpredictable nature of the English weather, which turned out to be as extreme in the spring of 1608 as it had been the winter before.

A Dutch sea captain had been found, and his ship chartered. William Brewster had felt confidence in the man from the moment they had met in Hull. At a quiet waterside inn, they had spent several hours poring over maps and finalising the arrangements, from an embarkation point in the Humber estuary to their arrival in Holland.

Early one morning, before dawn, the women and children left

Scrooby in three flat-bottomed boats, tightly packed with the Separatists' baggage and clothing, cooking pots and pans and livestock, including goats, chickens and geese. They paddled quietly down the River Idle until they came to the River Trent. Here they landed and boarded a 'barque', a small sailing boat, which was loaded from stempost to stern.

A Barque

In spite of all their preparation, nothing went according to plan. The River Trent was swollen from the ice and snow that had built up during the previous winter. The boat moved through the water with surprising speed, driven forward by spring currents and a brisk northwest wind. They arrived a day earlier than anticipated at the mouth of the Humber estuary and here, close to the North Sea, they encountered some very unpleasant weather. Steering as close to the coast as was possible, the captain could do nothing about the battering wind and turbulent waters. Within hours most of his passengers were being violently seasick.

The mood of optimism began to fade. Much of the barque was exposed to the elements. Squalls of rain added to their discomfort. Cold, wet and sick, the children and animals howled out their misery increasingly loudly. As the rain poured down and the boat rolled and pitched in the water, the situation was clearly getting out of hand. At this point, Bridget Robinson and Mary Brewster decided to tackle the situation and talk to the captain. It was decided that they simply could not face another twenty-four hours on the turbulent waters. Their best course would be to steer the boat into a creek, where it would be more sheltered, and thus reduce the discomfort of everyone on board.

Early in the morning of the next day, the Dutch vessel appeared at the appointed hour. By the time the sun was up, the sailing ship was clearly visible for many miles. The barque, however, was lying in low water and could not sail until the tide came in at midday.

Recognising the need for urgency, the Dutch captain lowered the long boat, and instructed his men to start picking up the party of

Separatists already gathered on the shore. He could see them from the ship, walking up and down on the shingle, anxiously waiting for their womenfolk to join them. The water was still choppy and the going was not at all easy. Eventually the ship's long boat arrived at the water's edge and eighteen men, William Bradford among them, were ferried back to the Dutch vessel.

The men quickly clambered on board, but just as the long boat was about to take off again, several things happened at once. On one side of the inlet, the barque full of women and children was bobbing along on the choppy water. On land, marching across the common and down the slope to the waters' edge, was an army platoon, complete with foot soldiers, guns and horses. It was clearly heading for the men standing on the bank.

The passengers, crew and captain of the Dutch ship watched the scene unfolding before them with horror. The captain, his face white, clenched his fist and slammed it against the side of the ship:

"Sacramente . . . Sacramente . . . Sacramente!"

Then, turning to the Pilgrims standing beside him, he demanded,

"What is this? What have you brought upon me? My ship will be destroyed and my men imprisoned. We must leave now . . . we are accursed!" He turned on his heel and barked a series of orders in Flemish to the first mate and the crew. Within minutes the anchor was raised, the sails hoisted and the sailing ship was making for the open sea.

In the barque, as it drew closer to the shore, and on land there was terrible panic. Women who had seen their menfolk board the departing Dutch ship became frantic. Where was the Dutch ship going? Would their husbands and their sons ever be seen or heard of again? Those left behind on land were just as desperate. Mary Brewster, standing at the front of the barque, was no more than a stone's throw from her husband as he waved frantically to her from the beach. She screamed:

"Fly! William Fly! Do not let them catch you. It will be the end!" Her pleas were taken up by many of the women on the barque, who began to shout, "Run! Run! Save yourselves!"

Above the roar of the waves, the men on the beach could hear the desolate cries of their wives and children carried on the wind. For a split second it seemed as though nobody knew what to do. The men on the beach stood transfixed at the sight of their women on the boat, so near and yet so far. At the same time the troops were now bearing down on them at great speed, and the men on the bank could see the officers on horseback and a sizeable contingent of foot soldiers, some carrying muskets and others running beside the horses hauling guns and carts.

"We can do nothing," shouted William Brewster to his companions.

"Do as they say, flee for your lives," and grabbing the hand of his fifteen-year old son Jonathan, he ran towards the trees and disappeared into the darkness beyond. Seeing their leader depart so swiftly, most of the men took off in various directions, skirting the common or running for cover towards the woods. Three of them stayed behind, choosing to remain with the women.

The King's troops were not quick enough to catch any of the men that ran off. The captain of the barque, however, handed his passengers over to the army as soon as he could, anxious to co-operate with the authorities. As for the soldiers, they wasted no time in arresting all the Separatists they could find. But it was hardly an impressive catch: instead of apprehending a group of violent religious extremists, the captain of the troops (who had had no previous dealings with the Separatists) found himself in charge of a band of wailing women and children. Shivering, miserable, and wet through, his captives came complete with piles of pots and pans, boxes of old clothes, bleating goats, and squawking chickens and geese.

The troops stood around, surprised and in some cases genuinely upset by what they saw: around fifty women, some with babes in arms, desperately distressed at the fate they believed awaited them – imprisonment, torture or worse. They were absolutely terrified. They had no idea how honourable or dishonourable the troops were, but after their previous attempt to escape, they were very wary. Sensing their mothers' fear and distress, the children were crying inconsolably.

With help from his soldiers and a makeshift raft, the captain of the troops let his prisoners gather their belongings. He then made them rest and eat. After things had calmed down (by which time it was evident that neither he nor his men meant any real harm), he packed the Separatists onto the carts and took them to various local prisons in and around Hull and Grimsby. Back in the towns the women found that the magistrates and local townsfolk were largely sympathetic to their situation. They were determined not to let them or their children languish in the same sordid conditions as hardened prisoners. Word had got out that the group was now homeless, and their menfolk had either been chased away or hunted down. Often they were treated with humanity, and even kindness.

As the weeks and months passed, the women became an increasing embarrassment to the judiciary and the army who didn't know what to do with them. They were certainly not guilty of any actual crime, and many thought that it was quite inappropriate to punish them at all. They were moved from one prison to another, with security becoming increasingly lax. Yet wherever they went, they found friends.

The women Separatists were widely regarded as brave and honourable, as indeed they were. In and out of prison, other women admired their moral courage, and it reinforced their own convictions. Their plight made a powerful impact on the consciousness of the people of England. Their gentleness, their open love and respect for the Bible and their special brand of Christianity contributed to a debate that grew steadily stronger as the years went by, expressing itself partly as a massive surge of interest in the Puritan movement. Meanwhile the authorities let the Separatist women and children go. Many of them had made friends or established contacts that enabled them to find temporary homes before being reunited with their loved ones in England or Amsterdam.

The fate of the others was altogether different. Those on board the Dutch sailing vessel were bound on a journey they would never forget, whilst those who had escaped the troops by land used their freedom to good effect. William Brewster had taken refuge in the house of a relative in Hull, where he was able to gather regular information about the welfare of his wife Mary and his daughters, Patience and baby Fear. Fortunately for him, all three had been imprisoned in Hull. With the help of Separatist sympathisers, he was able to send his family and the other imprisoned women gifts of food and money, which eased their situation considerably. He also made it his business to keep in contact with all the prisoners and to find out the whereabouts of every single Separatist who had escaped the troops. In this way he played a key role in reuniting all the families that had been involved in the attempt to escape.

William Brewster had learned his lesson. He now realised that the only way they could re-establish the community in Amsterdam would be by arranging for the brethren to make the crossing in small family groups, using the sailing ships that regularly plied the North Sea between the eastern ports and the Lowlands.

By now the Scrooby Separatists had become something of a *cause célèbre*. The King's secret service was hunting for Brewster high and low, but they could not track down the ex-post master of Scrooby. He was busy travelling between the North and the South of England, using his contacts and influence to raise funds to pay for the gradual exodus of Pilgrims from England to the Netherlands. He also used his powers of persuasion to enlist a number of new supporters destined to play an important part in the Pilgrims' future in Holland . . . and ultimately beyond.

Chapter

4 A NEW LIFE IN THE LOWLANDS

The eighteen Separatists who had climbed aboard the Dutch ship found themselves destitute, penniless and with nothing in the world except the clothes on their backs. Their last sight of England was of the army descending on their nearest and dearest. And they were about to discover (for the first time, but not the last) that the power of nature could be far more dangerous than any man-made force.

On that first day, the Pilgrims remained in the cabin that had been prepared for them below decks. A few hammocks had been strung up, but they soon found out that in heavy seas there was nowhere safe to rest. They sat cross-legged on the floor, slipping and sliding about as the ship rolled and pitched in a growing tempest. Five men had gone to the captain to plead with him to turn back and deposit them on the shore, but he made it quite clear that it was out of the question. Several of the Pilgrims were openly weeping.

"We have abandoned our wives and children. How can you be so hard-hearted?" sobbed Thomas White. The captain slammed his cabin door on them.

The next day the weather was a great deal worse. Huge waves and scudding clouds were all that could be seen, and so it remained for day after day. The passengers, who had never experienced anything like this before, stayed out of the way, praying and talking to each other. Half of them were extremely sea-sick. Their fears were further increased by the crew, who by

A storm at sea

now were visibly apprehensive.

By day three, the wooden ship was rolling and dipping through waves that were often almost as high as the main mast. Overnight, the storm reached new heights, and the Pilgrims rattled around in their cabin, clinging on to anything they could find, as immense seas hammered the tiny vessel. Suddenly a mountainous wave washed across the deck, breaking open the hold and flooding the cabin. In almost total darkness the Pilgrims staggered about, knee-deep in the water, blinded by the salt and soaked to the skin. Above the howling wind and the creaking and juddering of the ship they could hear the crew screaming and crying out in a variety of languages:

"God save us!"

"We are lost!"

"Help us, Lord, before we die!"

"I don't want to die!"

"We sink! We sink! All is lost!"

After they had bailed out as much water as they could, the Pilgrims held hands in the dark and prayed:

A contemporary Dutch merchant ship

"Lord, protect us and save us. We open our hearts to You in this storm and beg for Your mercy, O Lord who commands the tempest and the seas. We plead for Your grace and the protection of this ship and all its passengers. Watch over and save us. We are Your servants in life as in death . . ." And they prayed and prayed.

Powerless to do anything other than keep its head facing the oncoming waves, the Dutch ship was driven north and then east, towards the Norwegian coast. Mountainous seas continued to batter her for two more days, but then it grew calmer.

A week later, they sailed into the harbour at Amsterdam. Once again, they realised how close they had been to death. A crowd of kindly folk stood waving to them at the quayside, welcoming the newcomers to Holland. Many ships had been damaged or lost at sea during the previous fortnight, and those that had survived were thought to have been specially blessed by God. The captain, who had been so impatient at first, shook hands with the eighteen Pilgrims and wished them Godspeed.

Dishevelled, dirty and shaking, the Separatists stepped onto dry land, ready to begin their new life. But they immediately felt like strangers in a strange land. Few of them had even visited a busy city before. Here not only did the people speak a different language, but the sights, smells, sounds, even the light itself was different from anything they had experienced in their lives. The streets were thronged with people, rich and poor from many countries. Everywhere they walked they saw wonderful buildings more gracious and elegant than anything they had known in England.

Holland was at the height of its power – culturally, materially and politically. Amsterdam provided a home for all kinds of Protestant churches and the government prided itself on its open-mindedness and freedom of speech. Despite

The Port of Amsterdam

The Separatists learned a variety of trades

twenty-five years of war with Spain (now beginning to draw to a close), the country had grown enormously wealthy, and its ready acceptance of exiles and religious refugees had brought many new skills that contributed to the culture and economy in various ways.

There was work to be had, but for foreigners with little more than a knowledge of farm labour, much of it was poorly paid. The Dutch worked and traded in iron, silk, linen, lace and many different kinds of materials and textiles. All kinds of new buildings were under construction within and around the city – warehouses, palaces, houses, arsenals, docks and fortifications. For the first group of Pilgrims, as well as those that followed them in the ensuing weeks and months, Amsterdam was a city of sheer wonder.

Yet life was far from comfortable for the Separatists. They had to learn to speak Dutch as quickly as possible, otherwise they could not survive. They were forced to live on the edge of the city in poor housing – sometimes they had to camp out in unfinished buildings, and occasionally even in tents. Work was not always easy to find. Almost as soon as they arrived, they had sought the help of other English Separatist groups, of which two were already established in the city. The older of the two churches was the exiled Ancient English Church, headed by Francis Johnson. The second was run by John Smith, who had come from Gainsborough, twenty miles east of Scrooby. Many of the Scrooby Separatists knew John Smith, and had heard him preach. He had left England a year before William Bradford's arrival on the Dutch ship in April 1608.

In the summer and autumn that followed Bradford was delighted to find himself reunited with the entire congregation of the Scrooby Church. The last to arrive were William Brewster and John Robinson, who had stayed behind to care for the older and more vulnerable members of the Church, and help them on the journey to a new life, if they so wished.

Bradford wasted no time in getting to know Amsterdam and its people. He already knew many of the congregation of the Ancient Church, including their pastor Francis Johnson, their teacher Henry Ainsworth, the four ruling elders, the deacons and the deaconess. William particularly liked the deaconess, a stern-faced woman in her sixties with a heart of gold, who kept the children quiet during services and tended the sick. The young Pilgrim also made a point of keeping in touch with John Smith, who remembered him from his own visits to Scrooby Manor.

In between looking for work, Bradford also managed to fit in regular attendance at Church. When all the English Separatists gathered together, the congregation was some three hundred strong – they needed a good-sized meeting room. Bradford managed to avoid much of the gossip that flowed so freely amongst the English churchgoers. He knew that loud complaints had been made against Francis Johnson's wife, because she dressed in a colourful way and had a special fondness for large hats. There were also dark rumours of friendships between Separatists outside marriage, but he preferred not to listen to such scandal-mongering. Yet he could not avoid seeing that relations between the leaders of the various Separatist groups were not running smoothly, though it was not until December 1608 that he realised how serious the situation had become. By this time, William Brewster was living in a small workman's cottage on the edge of Amsterdam.

Bradford was invited to join the Brewster family for dinner, and he was delighted to find himself spending an evening with his mentor, and to pick up news of his friends from Scrooby.

After the meal of bread, fish, pickled fruit and beer, Brewster, his son Jonathan and William Bradford sat down by the fire, while Mary attended to Patience and Fear upstairs.

"I have something to tell you both," said Brewster, adding "but it cannot be spoken about again, until we meet with the brethren, and then they must decide."

The two young men nodded and remained silent.

"We appear to have arrived in Amsterdam at a time when the Separatist churches are not in harmony. The matters that are being discussed could place our flock in grave danger. Our moral virtue, our sanctity, our very faith are at risk."

He turned to young William.

"What is your impression of John Smith since he came to this country?"

"He seems different, there is no doubt. Perhaps he has lost some of his fire, yet I heard him talking openly and maybe even angrily against baptism with Henry Ainsworth and Richard Clifton."

"You are very observant, my young friend. It seems to me that he has chosen to walk in strange paths, and this can be seen when he preaches. He has arrived at convictions that I cannot share or uphold. His arguments against infant baptism will not be welcomed by our brotherhood, but a matter of even greater import is that he wishes the elders of the Church to be ordained, and given the authority to govern the congregation." He paused, and stared into the fire.

"Pastor Robinson, Henry Ainsworth and myself know that the government of the flock must be shared amongst the Church as a whole, and the congregation must determine its own future, otherwise it will be merely a matter of time before the Church returns to the old order that defends corruption amongst its leaders, the old order that endorses government by bishops within the Catholic and English Churches. Have we suffered imprisonment and a dozen other trials and tribulations to return to those very evils that we left behind?"

"No, most certainly we must not!" agreed the two young men.

"Pastor Robinson wants the brethren to be free to worship in a Church that is true to the spirit of Our Father and the holy scriptures, and respectful and protective of the flock. So we have to ask our brothers to consider whether we should not move to a city where we would no longer be threatened by the uncertainties and moral lapses of other groups, and the brethren would be free to hold prayers and preach the word of God as they think right, without these misguided doctrines."

"So we must move again?"

"If the congregation so agrees, yes. But this time it will not be such a difficult journey. It has been suggested that we go to Leiden, a fine city and a place of learning, which might suit us all very well."

"Certainly, after so many adventures, we need to find a home where we can worship in peace, with the blessing of Our Father. It seems that we cannot do so in Amsterdam."

"Wisely spoken," said William Brewster, and smiled at his young protégé.

A month later, Robinson and his congregation applied to the authorities of Leiden for permission to reside there and their application was accepted. The response to their application, dated February 1609, stated:

> *"The Court refuses no honest person entry or residence to this city, provided that such persons behave themselves, and submit to the laws and ordinances; and therefore the coming of the members of your institution will be both agreeable and welcome."*

A thirty-eight mile journey brought the Pilgrims to a city of 40,000 citizens that had suffered greatly during the war with Spain, and had lost much of its population in a siege some thirty years earlier. Since then, it had recovered and risen to become a city of culture and elegance. William Bradford was always to remember Leiden with great affection, later writing of it as "a fair and beautiful city, and of a sweet situation, but made more famous by the university wherewith it is adorned." It was a university town of such stature that Europe's finest minds were drawn to it, and there encountered some of the greatest scholars of the age. Leiden was central to Holland's renaissance: scarcely eighteen months earlier, one of the world's greatest artists,

Rembrandt

Rembrandt van Rijn, had been born there, the son of a mill owner.

For the next twelve years, Leiden served as the home for the hundred Scrooby Separatists, until the wheels of fortune began once more to turn for them. As always, many adventures befell them before they eventually decided that it was time for them to move on.

Chapter

5 THE CALL OF THE NEW WORLD

Between October 1573 and March 1574 the City of Leiden had been under a siege so horrific that the population had been reduced to eating rats. The town burgomaster had offered his body as food to his starving citizens rather than surrender to the Spaniards. Fortunately, his proposal had been refused, though it had strengthened the resolve of the people.

Afterwards, Holland's Prince William of Orange rewarded the community of Leiden for their bravery by offering them the choice of either living tax free, or having a University. They chose the latter, and in this way Holland's foremost Protestant university came into being.

The University was famous in the fields of philosophy, political science and above all, theology. The leading scholars of the different religious groups − Calvinists, Arminians and Anabaptists − were all known to John Robinson, and the pastor of the Separatists was well known to the scholars of the University. Indeed, if Robinson and his flock had not been such a thorn in the side of King James I of England, the pastor of the Scrooby Separatists would himself have held a University position. Political expediency alone had prevented John Robinson from gaining a professorship at the Dutch University. As time passed, resentments between the King and the Separatists were increasing.

Pastor Robinson's culture, intellect and powers of leadership were vital to the Separatists during their years in Leiden. The community had grown to around three hundred by 1617, and had attracted some clever and talented men, who were destined to play a vital part in the history of the pilgrims. Most important of these were Edward Winslow, Miles Standish, John Carver and Robert Cushman. Lesser personalities to emerge at this point in time were the physician Samuel Fuller, Degory Priest and Isaac Allerton, who married Brewster's pretty daughter Fear. A tailor from London, he joined the community and became a citizen of Leiden, later holding a position of some responsibility amongst them, though he lived to disappoint his father-in-law and the whole community.

The Scrooby Separatists encountered many difficulties on their arrival. They discovered that Leiden was an even harder place than Amsterdam when it came to finding work. A thriving port, Amsterdam always needed dockers, messengers and carriers. By contrast Leiden lay inland, and labourers had to adapt and learn local trades and skills to survive. Some joined the University, which enjoyed certain benefits such as immunity from police jurisdiction and exemption from billeting soldiers and military levies. Others applied for citizenship in order to gain admission to the trade guilds. The wool trade was the biggest employer in the city and many of the brethren took advantage of this. Among them was William Bradford, who had settled down to family life with the charming and impetuous Dorothy May. They had married on December 18, 1613, when Bradford was twenty-three.

Edward Winslow

Miles Standish

As for William Brewster, he had taken up teaching English, but at first things hadn't gone at all well for him. Finding a suitable home for his family was difficult since the rapidly growing population of Leiden had created something of a housing shortage. Newcomers had to accept whatever was offered, and the grimy little house in 'Stinksteeg' was not at all what Mary Brewster, by 1609 heavily pregnant again, had had in mind.

The town was surrounded by the River Rhine and just about every house was accessible by water. Although the population was committed to keeping Leiden scrupulously clean, some areas were definitely less healthy than others. Less than a week after the birth of their fourth child, William and Mary Brewster were mourning her death. It was hardly surprising that the family moved as soon as possible from that damp and reeking house to another in St Ursula's Lane. Eventually they came to settle in Choir Alley, close to St Peter's Church.

In due course most of the Separatists followed their leader to the same quarter of the city (near St Peter's Church) and there lived in peace for a number of years. With the help of his brother-in-law Ralph Tickens, William Jepson and Henry Wood, Pastor John Robinson had bought a property with some land in Bell Alley in 1611. In 1612 he moved there with his wife Bridget, and their six children and servant. Known as 'the House with the Green Door', it came to play a vital part in the lives of the Separatists for some fourteen years, serving both as church and meeting place, until Robinson's death on March 1, 1625.

William Brewster, meanwhile, was once again proving his ability to turn his hand to a number of skills. In addition to teaching, he had grown interested in the opportunities opened up by the printing trade – increasingly important as more men and women, including the Separatists, wanted to read the Bible. He set up his own printing works with the help of Thomas Brewer, an Englishman living in Leiden, with strong sympathy for the non-conformist movement, and wealthy enough to pay for a printing press.

Print technology played a crucial part in shaping history during those years. It was the printing of the Geneva Bible, after all, which had placed the teachings of God, Christ and his apostles in the hands of anyone who could read English. Now the printing press was to play an even more dramatic part in shaping the history of the Pilgrim Fathers. In the England of Elizabeth and James printing was strictly controlled by the state, and unlicensed publishing was not tolerated. England's monarchs feared that freedom of expression would threaten the stability of Church and State, so any printing presses, other than those authorised in London, Edinburgh, Dublin, Oxford and Cambridge, were illegal. As the monarch and the bishops controlled and censored everything that was printed, anything published about the Separatists took the form of attacks, libellous criticisms of them and their ideas that were bitterly resented by the Pilgrims. In Holland such censorship did not exist and some of the disillusioned exiles were determined to put their side of the argument.

Brewster now began to print a great variety of books and pamphlets, many of them sharply critical of the Church of England. These volumes did not state where they had been printed, so their source could not be traced . . . at first.

Life in Leiden was not growing easier for the Brethren. Many of them had visited both Pastor Robinson and Elder Brewster, in utter despair at the hardships they faced in their daily lives. In the spring of 1617 a special meeting was called at "the House with the Green Door". Some sixty Separatists attended, young and old alike. John Langmore, a young cloth worker, was the first to speak:

"Brothers, I urge you to consider whether we should not quit this place. We work day and night, as do our wives and children, yet our wages barely pay for our food, and there is no way that we can save for our own future or that of our children. Since he moved here, my father has become a sick man, and I have to care for him as well. Now I know why Pastor Clifton chose to stay in Amsterdam. This place is neither healthy for us, nor kind to us. I cannot think of anything that I may look forward to, either for myself or my children, as long as we remain in Leiden. It is only the presence of the Brethren and my love of the good Lord that keeps me here." A great many voices could be heard muttering in agreement.

Thomas White, a carpenter, stood up.

"I believe in the goodness and wisdom of the Brethren, but I also believe that the Lord has better places in the world where we might live and work in peace and happiness. We call this place 'home' but we are strangers here. Less than eighteen months ago, my four nephews all left home to work as sailors and soldiers because there was no work for them here in Leiden. They all spoke Dutch, and might have passed as Dutchmen. Over a year has passed and none of them has returned. Our young people no longer wish to stay with the community, and we cannot blame them, yet how is the community to survive if our young people leave us to seek their fortune elsewhere?"

Cries of 'True' and 'Yes!' could be heard all around. Richard Hooke, one of the older Separatists at the meeting turned to John Robinson.

"Pastor Robinson, it is not in my heart to complain, since you and Elder Brewster have cared for us, your flock, as loving parents, and I have come to know the love of our Father through your love. We have our crosses to bear, and our sorrows, and it is true what Brother White says, that the young will leave us for a life that is easier, if it is only to find the means to feed and live. As the Lord loves us and protects us, we should surely plan to find for ourselves a place where we might work and live, without those temptations that take away our young people. This must be the way ahead." Shouting across the murmuring voices, Hooke's brother William yelled out, "Pastor Robinson, how can we live and worship in the name of Our Father in a godless land where there is no respect for the Sabbath?' Another great murmur of agreement could be heard, and John Robinson nodded his head approvingly and replied:

"I do not deny that there are many reasons for us to seek a new life elsewhere. It is true, the people of Holland do not respect the Sabbath in the same way as our community does, and that there are temptations for young people everywhere. But if we were to move on, where should we find a country that would provide a good home for us and our women and children?"

At this point, John Carver, a man with some knowledge of trade and worldly affairs, stood up and spoke:

"Pastor Robinson, since I first heard rumours of further possible wars here in Holland (wars which would not be of our choosing, but would surely involve us), I have been making enquiries about other lands where we might dwell in peace." He added, "– the best opportunities for us lie either in the land known as New Guyana in the South of America, or else New England in the North of that place."

The debate suddenly became very noisy and animated, and Thomas Collins, who had worked as a sailor and had been captured by pirates, spoke with great passion against any plan to go to the South Americas. According to him New Guyana was a country where the Brethren would suffer terribly from every kind of disease and pestilence, in the most terrible heat. Worse still, the natives of those parts had no love for strangers, and were known to devise terrible tortures for them – mutilation and even cannibalism. The meeting began to voice a preference for New England.

"It is true," said John Carver, "that the climate of that place is much closer to our own."

A voice now spoke from the back of the crowed room. It was Elder Brewster, and the brothers turned to listen to his deep, resonant tones:

"Brothers, we must find a new home, where we may bring up our children safely and advance the Kingdom of God, as we and the Lord see fit. The time has come to find a blessed place where we can settle permanently in a land where all our hopes and aspirations may be made possible." Pastor Robinson nodded in agreement.

It was then decided that Robert Cushman and John Carver would journey to England to seek out men and companies who would be willing to finance such a venture. Once more the Separatists were destined to learn the hard lessons of experience; not the least of these was how much the King of England feared and disliked them.

6 The Struggle to Set Out

With so little money or influence, the Separatists were destined to be exploited by the ruthless speculators planning to invest in the New World. For the next two years, they struggled to gain the funding and permissions needed to set up a colony in New England, but their efforts were constantly thwarted. A new and sinister figure, Thomas Weston, now appeared on the scene, while William Brewster's final slap in the face for the King and the bishops nearly cost him his life.

Night after night the Separatists pored over the latest books extolling the virtues of New England as a place to live and cultivate the land. Recent volumes included "A Description of New England," "Nova Britannia Offering Most Excellent Fruits by Planting in Virginia," and "A Brief and True Relation of the Discoverie of the Northern Part of Virginia: Being a Most Pleasant Fruitful and Commodious Soile."

These avidly read books were the travel brochures of their day, and were every bit as 'creative' in content. They were designed to encourage people to settle in new lands, and so carefully avoided describing the real hardships that confronted new arrivals in America. From these books, the Separatists were led to believe that they would soon be trading in whale oil, furs, silk, minerals, herbs, tobacco and timber.

Some of the less open-minded Brethren were still unhappy about the possible move. They feared oppression from the existing colonists, and they also feared the unknown – and not without reason.

The two Separatist deacons, John Carver and Robert Cushman, visited the offices of the Virginia Company in London, the company that controlled trade and colonisation in New England. They were treated with kindness and respect by Company officials, who (like many after them) realised that the Separatists would make a good investment as future colonists. It would be hard to find such an honourable, God-fearing and committed work force anywhere. The controllers of the Virginia Company encouraged the Separatists to believe that it would not be difficult to get the King's permission to set out, but they were quite wrong. The King opposed their application on the grounds of the Pilgrims' religious beliefs.

Carver and Cushman returned despondently to Leiden and put together a document with seven articles of faith signed by Pastor Robinson and Elder Brewster. Back in England, they took this document to the Privy Council, but failed to gain the necessary confidence of the authorities.

Using all the influence he could muster, Elder Brewster took off for England and petitioned one of the leading figures in the Virginia Company, Sir Edwin Sandys, who obliged him by presenting a private motion to the King via the Secretary of State. For one exhilarating moment Brewster thought they were home and dry. The King had agreed, subject to approval by the bishops. Then the Separatists learned that the Privy Council would also have to grant them a patent. They were back to square one.

Brewster was a busy man. He did not stay long in London. He had recently contracted to print a number of books that he knew would prove important. Among these were two by a Scotsman, David Calderwood, attacking the system of government of the Anglican church by bishops just at the moment when King James, King of England and Scotland, was trying to impose bishops on the Presbyterian Church of Scotland (which, like the Separatist Church, was ruled by systems of elders).

The publication of Calderwood's two books created quite a storm. While many of the people of Scotland were delighted, Calderwood, Brewster, and his business partner, Brewer, were soon running for their lives from King James's men.

Printers at work

The King's agents worked out by a process of deduction exactly where the book had been printed. By this time King James was seriously annoyed with the Separatists and their activities. He gave orders to his secret service to track down any individual associated with the publication of the books. The Dutch had no desire to set up embarrassing political tensions and they would probably have agreed to hand over Brewer and Brewster there and then, had it not been for the fact that Brewer turned out to be a member of the University of Leiden. This privilege gave Brewster's partner some protection, and held up the process of search and arrest.

When the warrant was finally issued, the attic in Brewster's house in Bell Alley was forcibly searched and found to contain a large number of unauthorised books, printing materials, type and ink. The room was sealed off and the authorities were given the go-ahead to find and detain William Brewster. But once again the Separatist leader had managed to give the King's men the slip, and from this time onward, he was nowhere to be found despite vigorous searches that spanned both Holland and England. His absence was to prove most unfortunate for the Separatists, but as a man on the run, he was obliged to stay well away from all further negotiations. Indeed, he was obliged to keep a low profile for the ensuing months.

Meanwhile Cushman and Carver were determined to find an organisation that would support their scheme. Two opportunities arose – one from the New Netherlands Company, and another from an opportunistic London merchant, one Thomas Weston. This wily and hardened businessman set out to discourage the Separatists from doing a deal with the New Netherlands Company, arguing that the Dutch were unreliable as business partners. Despite his lack of experience in such deals, Weston proceeded to put together a consortium of merchants to finance the project.

Acquainted with the Pilgrims through Edward Pickering (who was married to a Separatist), Weston now worked his way into the favour of the Brethren, intending to gain the trust of Pastor Robinson. On various visits to Leiden he sat in the Pastor's garden, enlarging on how he intended to provide shipping and money for the voyage, with the minimal contractual arrangements.

In reality, Weston was trying to gauge the Separatists' financial commitment to the project. He carefully drew up an initial contract which

The Old Library, Leiden University

specified a joint stock arrangement for seven years with shares fixed at £10 for every participant over sixteen. The workers (or Planters as they were called) had to serve their masters, the investors (Adventurers) for five days a week in order to repay their debts. When the contract expired, the capital and accumulated profits would go to the Adventurers, but the Planters would retain the houses and the gardens that they had cultivated.

Once again the goodness and honesty of the Separatists strongly recommended the project to investors. There were around seventy of these, and quite a number of them were already sympathetic to the non-conformist cause.

Once Weston realised how desperate the Separatists were to leave, he started to change the arrangements concerning the negotiations and the contract. All contractual bargaining would now take place in London, and only Cushman would be involved. Pastor Robinson grew increasingly anxious. He did not trust Weston and strongly believed that Robert Cushman was not up to the task of negotiating with such a hard-bitten business man. Elder Brewster was now sorely missed, but he was nowhere to be found.

Pastor Robinson was right, as usual. The contract was changed, and the final version was far less favourable to the Separatists in every respect, particularly with regard to the house and land arrangements. A clause insisting upon two days of rest had also been removed. The Pilgrims would now be expected to work seven days a week.

Once more the Separatists found themselves in a position of weakness, for, apart from being out of their depth when it came to business dealings, they had already committed themselves. William Bradford, Thomas Rogers and Robert Cushman had all sold their houses to help finance the voyage and Thomas Weston knew this.

In the summer of 1620, Robert Cushman, fearful that the project would fail, agreed to sign the revised contract that Thomas Weston placed before him. Weston had achieved what he wanted. Cushman had been outmanoeuvred. Desperate to keep all sides happy, Cushman managed to annoy everyone, and couldn't work out why. He did not operate well under pressure, and was failing to defend the Pilgrims' cause. Fearful that the Brethren would condemn him for signing the unfavourable contract, Cushman decided not to tell anyone what he had done.

What had become widely known was that the Pilgrims were planning a voyage. A growing number of Separatists, in Amsterdam, London and Essex, now wanted to join the expedition. As the potential passenger list increased, another agent was brought in – Christopher Martin. Keen to get going, Martin and John Carver went ahead and ordered provisions in Southampton, which infuriated Weston and Cushman in London, who saw this as an act of interference.

Yet in spite of their disagreements, progress was being made on no less than three fronts – London, Southampton and Leiden. But the financial side of the undertaking was looking less successful by the day. A number of investors who had initially shown interest now pulled out.

The harbour at Delfshaven

Weston was infuriated. He was becoming increasingly bullying and had threatened to pull out himself on more than one occasion. Letters flew backwards and forwards between England and Holland. It was a race against time, and the summer was slipping by. The Leiden Separatists let it be known that they were looking for a small ship to buy, which Weston considered a mistake. Ultimately his advice turned out to have been right, but the Separatists seemed doomed to learn the hard way.

A 60 ton ship, the *Speedwell*, was bought and moored in Delfshaven; it was thought that she would be useful for fishing and trading. Meanwhile in London a 180 ton ship, the *Mayflower*, had been hired.

As the time for departure approached, the community and individual families had to make hard decisions, about who would and who would not be going. William Brewster, still living in hiding, was now able to meet and talk to his wife regularly. They decided to make the voyage together with their two youngest sons, Love and Wrestling, aged nine and six. Jonathan Brewster (who was now twenty-seven) agreed to stay behind in Leiden in the house in Choir Alley, with his sister Patience, who had just turned nineteen, and Fear, a lively thirteen year-old.

William Bradford and his vivacious wife Dorothy took the painful decision to leave behind their beloved son John, who was barely two. The toddler would stay with Pastor and Bridget Robinson until such time as he could safely join his parents. Dorothy was bereft, but tearfully agreed that it was all for the best. Others chose to make the voyage without their wives, hoping that they would join them with their children later, when the plantation was established. These included Samuel Fuller, Richard Warren, and Francis Cooke.

21 July 1620, the day of departure from Leiden, was memorable for everyone involved. In the morning they rose early and went to pray. Pastor Robinson stood before them, wise and kindly. He had chosen his text with care, from the prophet Ezra, as he led the children of Israel out of captivity to Jerusalem:

'*And there, at the river, by Ahava, I proclaimed a fast, that we might humble ourselves before our God, and seek of Him a right way for us, and for our children, and for all our substance.'*

They prayed as never before, and many of them openly wept. Then they made their way, by boat from Leiden to Delfshaven, where the *Speedwell* had been made ready. The crowd that came to see them off included family members left behind, their dearest friends and the many friends they had made in Amsterdam. They spent the night quietly in port, eating, drinking and talking long into the night, anticipating all the adventures they might encounter, from pirates to storms and sea serpents. The following morning they awoke early, frightened and excited, ready for the great sea voyage ahead of them.

The memory of their moment of departure never left the Pilgrims. Those who were present remembered that day forever. Nearly everyone cried. They didn't know if they would ever see each other again, and for many of them, looking back, it was the last time they set eyes on their friends and relatives, young and old. For those who sailed on the *Speedwell*, it was the last time they would ever hear the reassuring voice of Pastor Robinson or see the little faces of beloved children – sons, daughters, nieces and nephews. Dorothy Bradford cried and cried when she saw baby John waving to her in the arms of Bridget Robinson.

When, many years later William Bradford came to write about that day, he even remembered the strangers, the Dutch men and women who had come to wave them off, and who had also been moved to weep.

On the quayside, amidst a crowd of loving friends and family, Pastor Robinson sank to his knees, with tears streaming down his face. He prayed to God to give the voyaging Pilgrims His blessing. The ship slid down the quayside, and they waved and waved, a band of pioneers destined to face dangers, joys and sorrows that they could not even imagine.

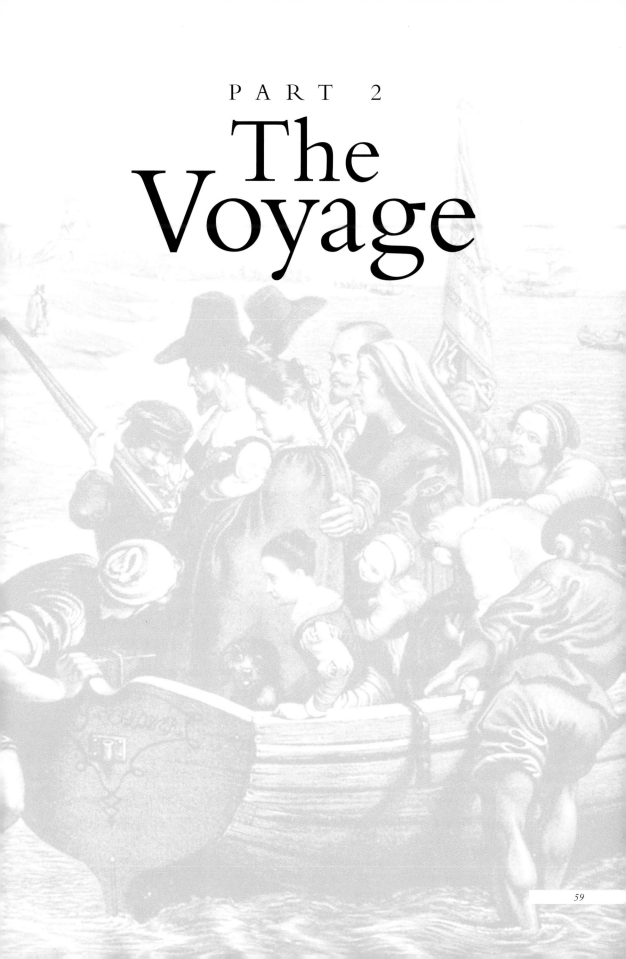

PART 2

The Voyage

7 THE *MAYFLOWER* HOISTS SAIL

The *Speedwell* made good progress during a late July week of blue skies, scudding clouds and strong south-westerly winds. The days were warm and the sun shone for much of the time. The fair weather and calm seas raised the hopes and spirits of the Pilgrims, after the sadness of their departure from Holland.

They arrived in Southampton towards the end of July. It was a warm, fine evening, and there was great excitement when they discovered that the *Mayflower* was already in harbour. A group from the *Speedwell* boarded the larger vessel that evening and was duly impressed to see how clean and shipshape she was. They were also pleased to find old friends and some new acquaintances ready to embark from England.

Making the most of the balmy summer weather Master Christopher Jones, the captain, took pleasure and pride in showing the visitors (Brewster, Bradford, Edward Winslow and Steven Hopkins) over his fine sailing ship. In conversation, he explained to them that it had originally been used for trade in the Baltic ports, and particularly in Norway. He thought the Brethren had chosen an excellent vessel for their venture. The *Mayflower* was a "sweet" ship, he explained, due to the cargo she had been carrying. Before he had acquired a share in her, she had traded in tar, lumber, and fish, but more recently she had sailed the Mediterranean seas and traded in herbs, spices, oil and wine.

As the quarters on ship were very cramped, many of the *Speedwell*'s passengers took the opportunity to visit Southampton, and stretch their legs on land while they could. In any case, the *Mayflower* was hardly peaceful: a troupe of carpenters were busy building bunks, shelves and also supports for the shallop, the small sailing boat that was housed as a series of component parts on the gun deck. The air rang with the sound of slapping waves, sawing, hammering and shouting, mingled with the cries of the seagulls. On the poop deck some sailors were mending sails, and singing merrily as they worked.

William Brewster turned to Master Jones and Robert Cushman, "When will we be ready for departure, for there are several good reasons why I, at least, should not tarry a moment longer than necessary."

"For my part," said the captain, "We could leave on the morrow."

"Then we must meet with Mr Thomas Weston and discuss the contract we have signed with that gentleman and the Adventurers," said Cushman quietly. "Mr Weston is expected from London by coach tomorrow afternoon." William Brewster was visibly uneasy with the delay, but agreed that the contract must be seen and approved by all of them.

The next day their leaders sat down in the captain's cabin on the *Mayflower*, waiting for the arrival of Thomas Weston.

Eventually the merchant strolled in and sat down, evidently pleased to find the gathered company waiting patiently for him. He greeted them all most affably, particularly Robert Cushman who had become increasingly agitated while they had been waiting for Weston.

"Good sirs, I have brought with me the new articles which have been copied most carefully into the new agreement," and he unfolded a large paper, adding "It has been signed by Master Cushman and myself, and now needs little more than the signatures of a few good men."

"I was not aware that there were new articles. Are we here to sign a different agreement from that shown to Pastor Robinson in June?" enquired William Brewster, looking hard at Robert Cushman, who had turned pale and was biting the nail of his little finger.

"You may also sign gentlemen, if you so wish, and then so will the

Adventurers, and then we are 'all shipshape and Bristol fashion', as the sailors like to say, and you are free to sail away to a new home and a better life," replied Weston, smiling broadly and showing a great many yellowed and broken teeth.

William Brewster and William Bradford sat down at the captain's table, holding the contract between them. After a while the gathered company heard a sharp intake of breath from Brewster, and then another. Bradford cleared his throat and then whispered something in Elder Brewster's ear, pointing to some words on the document.

"I have seen it, brother," said Brewster in a low growl. After three long minutes, Elder Brewster broke the silence, his voice scarcely concealing his anger.

"This contract has been changed . . . changed very greatly. The words relating to the Planters' rights to their homes, and indeed the days that they must work are entirely different from those in the draft contract shown to me by Pastor Robinson. It now appears that you expect the Planters to work without a sabbath, for there is no mention of one day of rest, let alone two. What say you, brother William, to this piece of paper?"

"Our brothers would never agree to such a contract . . . of this I am certain," replied Bradford. "Would you agree to it, Mr Carver?" John Carver took the paper from Bradford's hands and examined it closely.

"I had not realised that any such changes had been made. I have been in Southampton, as you know, working with Mr Martin and seeing to the ordering of provisions for the voyage. I would never have agreed to such . . . obligations. But you, Brother Cushman, you must know something of this since it bears your signature, and is dated July 5, yet you have not told a single soul amongst us that a new contract had been drawn up."

Robert Cushman said nothing, but chewed his fingernails. There was a long silence.

"What do you say to this, Brother Cushman?" asked Elder Brewster in a soft voice. Cushman frowned and continued to bite his nails. Brewster went on, "You knew of this. You signed this pact which favours the interests of the Adventurers at the expense of the Planters. According to this new contract, the houses and lands of the Planters will be divided, and all that they have achieved will be consigned to the common stock, leaving the Planters with nothing. And the days of rest . . . How came you to sign such a harsh and ungenerous document?"

Weston butted in:

"I object to your use of language, sir. This contract is most generous. It will give lasting employment to your people and indeed all the money needed to set up a new colony, to boot. This contract provides the means to give the Planters everything they could ever want for!"

"I am not addressing myself to you, Mr Weston. I wish to know how Mr Cushman came to sign such an agreement, without the knowledge or approval of our good Pastor!"

"I signed the deed in the best interests of all concerned," said Robert Cushman.

"There you are!" said Weston triumphantly, "he knows what's best!" "Hush, sir," said Brewster, "I ask you again, Brother Robert, how came you to sign this without the knowledge of Pastor Robinson?"

"If I had refused to sign, you would all be in Holland still – and perhaps you, William Brewster, would have been in the King's prison and not on board this ship. There would be no ships, no Planters, no Adventurers. I did this for the best. We have come so far, and we will continue our progress with the blessing of the good Lord. You and yours and all of our families were always my first concern, for I knew that nothing would come of it if I wasted days arguing, as we are doing now, over petty details. It is thanks to me that we are all ready to set sail, thanks to me and no one else!"

"Indeed, we are not ready to set sail at all, unless the Brethren here agree with you that this contract is acceptable. Brothers, I ask you to look at it with care, and tell me if you support it." The paper was passed around and then handed back to William Bradford who said:

"I for one will not support such a contract."

"Nor I, " said John Carver,

"Nor I, " said Christopher Martin,

"Nor I," said Edward Winslow,

"Nor I," said Stephen Hopkins.

"You have heard us all, Mr Weston. What say you to this?" demanded Elder Brewster. The merchant was purple in the face with rage.

"I should have known better than to waste my time with such a pack of stiff-necked bigots. You have wasted my time and that of many good men with your tedious complaints . . . And what have you got now, eh? Without me, you have nothing! Go forth and travel the world with nothing but a dry peascod and a ship's biscuit, and see how you fare on your own!"

"Mr Weston," pleaded Robert Cushman, "I am sure that you can contrive a contract that the Brethren would sign. So much is lost if this contract is cast aside."

"You are a fool, Robert Cushman – you and all your kind," barked Weston, standing up and kicking back the chair he had sat on. He picked up his cloak and hat and stomped towards the door. There, he turned on his heel:

"Go forth and stand on your own legs, and may the devil go with you!" and he stormed out of the cabin, slamming the door behind him.

The Pilgrims were still contracted to Thomas Weston and those Adventurers that had invested in the project. Nevertheless without the financial support of the agreement and the consortium of merchant Adventurers they were in serious trouble. With the passing of each day spent on English shores, William Brewster was becoming increasingly uneasy, for as long as the Separatists were docked in Southampton he risked being arrested, and this time it would mean certain death. The government had recently executed several notable Separatist and Puritan dissidents as a warning to others.

Decisions had to be made quickly. In the end the Pilgrims determined to sell off as much valuable goods and cargo as they could spare, beginning with a large quantity of butter. At the same time, they drafted a letter to the Adventurers, saying how sorry they were about the dispute, explaining their objections and offering the investors further incentives, but their new proposals were refused. While this was going on they were working hard to make up the missing finances by continuing to sell off more butter and oil and as many goods as they could manage without, leaving themselves with the minimum in terms of provisions, armour, muskets and even some basic necessities.

Spurred on by the wish to leave England as quickly as possible, and an encouraging letter from Pastor Robinson bidding them to proceed, they organised themselves as best they could between the two ships. A governor was appointed to each one, with the job of managing the provisions and their distribution.

As they set sail later that August, they did not realise that they were destined once again to be the victims of unscrupulous exploitation.

This time it was Captain Reynolds, master of the *Speedwell*, who proved treacherous and self-seeking. Knowing that the ship was carrying too large a mast for its size, and realising that this gave the impression that all was not as it should be, Reynolds waited for his moment. Almost as soon at the two ships had sailed from Southampton, he began to complain that the *Speedwell* was leaking dangerously. Seeing that Cushman was in a state of some anxiety, he played upon his fears, and soon word went round that the ship was "as leaky as a sieve." They turned the ships around and returned to Dartmouth for repairs. But in harbour, nothing much could be found to be wrong with her. They set off once again.

But Reynolds was now determined to extricate himself and his crew from the venture as soon as possible. He had been hired to stay on in the colony for a year, and it was thought that he feared that with the provisions so heavily cut, those on the smaller ship would come off worst. Perhaps he simply did not have the courage to face such a dangerous journey.

After they had turned round and returned to England yet again, the leaders of the expedition decided that there was no alternative but to leave the *Speedwell* behind, since its captain seemed to think it unseaworthy. In reality she was to continue sailing for many years to come, after her mast had been refitted. Reynolds had skilfully deceived the Separatists.

And so eventually, on the morning of 16 September 1620, the *Mayflower* finally sailed out of Plymouth harbour. Those making the journey had been carefully selected; twenty others, in poor health or with too many children to support, returned to Holland and England. Amongst them was Robert Cushman and his family. He claimed that the stress and suffering he had undergone during the months of negotiations had made him ill, and he was now deeply disillusioned with the whole enterprise.

The *Mayflower* had taken on board as much of the supplies from the *Speedwell* as it could carry. The summer was over. Finally, after thirteen years in the wilderness, the Pilgrims had set out on the journey they had always hoped to make, the journey to the new Jerusalem where they would live and worship in freedom. They had no idea of the trials that still awaited them.

Above: A cross section of the Mayflower
Opposite: The Mayflower *sails from Southampton*

Chapter

8 LIFE AT SEA

They had now been at sea for twenty days and things had changed greatly since they first set out. In the early days of the expedition they had walked the decks of the *Mayflower* full of cheerfulness. The sea had been calm, the waves glinting in the late summer sunshine. Now autumn was rapidly advancing and Southampton, Dartmouth and Plymouth were far behind them. Their clothes were sticky, the monotonous diet was bad for their health and the increasingly rough seas were making them sick. With each day that passed, they grew less optimistic.

The *Mayflower* carried 102 passengers: forty of them were committed Separatists, the rest were crew (of whom there were 25) and hired servants, plus extras, like their paid military leader, Miles Standish. At first there were considerable differences between the Pilgrims and the rest, in vision and aspiration. The Pilgrims planned to set up a Christian community in the New World based on their strong ideals and passionately held beliefs. They were known as the 'Saints' while the non-Separatists became the 'Strangers'. The Saints' unswerving faith in God made them more cheerful and stoical than the Strangers, who complained more often and were more inclined to question the wisdom of journeying into the unknown.

Amongst the Strangers there were a number of paid servants who worked for John Carver, Edward Winslow, Isaac Allerton, Samuel Fuller, Christopher Martin and Stephen Hopkins. Some families also took charge of stray orphans, virtually adopting them. Among those who took on such responsibilities were Deacon John Carver, William and Mary Brewster and Edward and Mary Winslow. Each of these families took in one of three children abandoned by their parents, three pale, sad-faced little creatures – Jasper, Richard and Ellen More.

In terms of their living quarters, diet and daily routine, there were few differences between the various passengers. Some cabins and sleeping areas were a little more comfortable than others. The marginally better living spaces had slightly wider bunks and a little more privacy than the others. These were positioned below the poop deck at the back of the ship and those using this cabin enjoyed the best light, and were located higher up than those crammed beneath the main deck. In the larger, less salubrious 'tween deck cabin, the swell of the sea could be felt much more strongly.

The Pilgrims at sea

Bunks had been bought for a price, and constructed by the ship's carpenters. Those that had more money could expect a little more space. In and around the 'tween deck cabin, the occupants had to share a dark and smelly area crammed full of boxes, bunks, trunks and hammocks, with no more than a curtain to give the womenfolk a little privacy. The dismembered pieces of the shallop also took up space in this main deck cabin. In and around its various component parts, the remaining area was narrow and uncomfortable. Travellers who could not afford bunks laid out their bedding as best they could on the boards.

The ship itself had never been designed for passengers, but then no passenger craft existed at that time. It was pretty uncomfortable for all of them and wherever one went, it was impossible to escape the sights, sounds and smells of other people.

In general, the crew were kind and helpful to the passengers, particularly to the women and children, with the exception of one gangly lad, Thomas North, who was gratuitously vicious to those who were seasick. As the weather worsened, it was as much as the Pilgrims could do to keep down their daily ration of hard biscuit, dried meat, pickle and soupy water or beer. North would taunt them mercilessly, threatening them with all manner of horrible fates, from being eaten by sea beasts, to falling in the sea while vomiting:

"Or better still, being thrown in by my own hand, for your vile weakness and foul stench."

If anybody dared to ask him to go away, North became even more threatening. Many of the women and children were afraid of him. With his wild staring eyes and grinning yellow face, he made the discomfort and embarrassment of seasickness even more unpleasant. Captain Jones reprimanded him more than once, but it only seemed to fuel his hatred and contempt of the sickly passengers.

As the days became perceptibly shorter, the seas became more turbulent and more passengers were ill. Calm seas and sunshine grew rarer. On the evening of the twentieth day, the wind and sea whipped up to a sudden storm in the space of a couple of hours. By the time the sun had gone down, there was nothing visible except the huge, foam-flecked waves; none of the passengers dared to go on deck. Captain Jones had lowered every sail, and was steering as best he could in the face of a series of cross winds and unpredictable squalls. The *Mayflower* bobbed helplessly on the waters like a toy ship.

As night drew on, the noise of howling wind and battering waves rose to a climax. In the dark, cold hull of the ship, the passengers clung to one other, praying and talking. A few sung, but their voices sounded weak and sad amidst the creaking of the ship and the roaring of the sea, so they gave up. Suddenly a series of massive waves struck the *Mayflower*. The ship gave a deep groan, and the passengers in the cabin below the main deck were showered with all sorts of rubble and dust. Soon afterwards, water started to seep in from the deck overhead, dripping on them, leaving them wet, cold and shivering with fear in their bunks.

With the dawn, calm was restored. The storm died down almost as quickly as it had blown up, much to everyone's joy. Elder Brewster called on the Brethren to offer up a prayer of thanks to God. His suggestion was readily accepted and the company gathered on the upper deck, damp and somewhat daunted by their experience, but more than ready to give praise to God, their protector, offering up their hearts and voices in gratitude for calmer seas.

Brewster's choice of text was particularly appropriate. He chose Psalm 107, which they sang together, in harmony. As the men, women and children intoned the words, tears rolled down many cheeks, especially those of the women, who wondered if their little ones would ever live to tell the tale of their strange and frightening journey.

They that go down to the sea in ships,

and occupy by the great waters,

They see the works of the Lord,

and his wonders in the deep.

For he commandeth and raiseth the stormy wind,

and it lifteth up the waves thereof.

They mount up to the heaven,

and descend to the deep

so that their soul melteth for trouble.

They are tossed to and fro,

and stagger like a drunken man,

and all their cunning is gone.

Then they cry unto the Lord in their trouble,

and he bringeth them out of their distress.

He turneth the storm to calm,

so that the waves thereof are still.

When they are quieted,

they are glad

and he bringeth them unto the haven,

where they would be.

After a brief prayer, Elder Brewster spoke to a few of the Pilgrims, enquiring after their health. He singled out Elizabeth Hopkins to find out how she was, following the previous night's storm. She was due to give birth within the next few weeks.

"Have you decided on a name?" he asked her.

"If the child is born at sea and a girl, Oceana, and if a boy, Oceanus. If born on land, we are undecided."

"May God's love go with you and your young ones, Sister Hopkins," he said, patting the head of her bright-eyed toddler, Damaris, clutching her mother's wrist.

During the prayers, Brewster had been somewhat distracted. As he glanced across the deck, he happened to notice the Captain, Master Jones, and his carpenter, Richard Bird, busily engaged in examining the ship's deck, with an expression of concentration and even concern on both their faces. They were down on their hands and knees and appeared to be chipping away at the deck with some small tools. After the congregation had dispersed, William Brewster walked over to the ship's Captain.

"Good morrow, Master Jones."

"And good day to you, Mr Brewster. A very pleasant rendition of the Lord's psalm. We are all moved by the sweet voices of the Brethren. However, you find us now on our hands and knees not so much in supplication as seeking to discover the truth, which we fear is not as pretty as we could have wished."

"How so, Master Jones?"

"Look at the boards and tell me what you see, good sir." Brewster bent down and peered at the planks of the deck.

"I see the wood of the ship, no more, no less."

"Indeed sir, this is true. But it is what you do not see that is my concern."

"How so?"

"Because between the planks there should be oakum – that is what we call the rope fibres and tar that we use to caulk . . . to seal . . . the deck and keep it watertight. But as you see, here there is no sign of the caulking."

"Why is that?"

"Why, indeed. The oakum seems to have been dislodged and fallen through into the cabin below, and if that is the case, I fear the worst. But I cannot be sure until we go below and find exactly what has caused this displacement."

"May I join you in this voyage of exploration?"

Above: *The Guildhall at Boston and the cells in which the Separatists were imprisoned*

Above: A View of Leiden in the 17th Century

Below: The Exchange at Amsterdam

Above: King James I was no friend to the Separatists

Above: *The Pilgrims depart from Plymouth for the* Mayflower

Below: *The* Mayflower *at sea*

Above: Map showing the town of Plymouth in New England where the Mayflower Pilgrims settled

Below: The Mayflower, *an early twentieth century representation*

Above*: Every man on the* Mayflower *signed the Compact*

Below*: 'One large whale inspected the tiny ship and chose to bask beside it at a distance'*

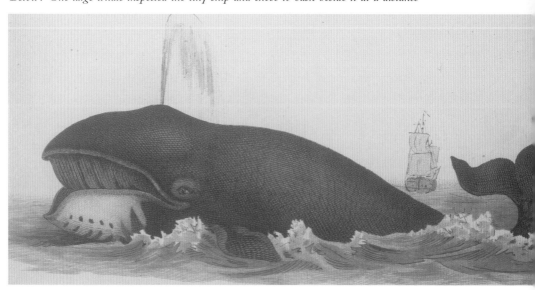

Above: The Pilgrims give thanks to God for their safe arrival

Below: Signing the Declaration of Independence

Above: *Massasoit of the Pokanokets comes in friendship*

Below: *The Lord is my Shepherd, I shall not want*

"Pray, do," said the ship's captain, getting to his knees and dusting off his breeches. He continued,

"There is another issue that concerns Mr Bird and myself. It is a matter of noise. To our ears, the ship is not singing as sweetly as usual. We fear that she may have taken some harm, as a result of last night's storm."

They climbed down through the hatch to the 'tween deck cabin where the carpenter lit a lantern. Here they made their way carefully through the ranks of bunks and boxes. A small circle of children were gathered around Edward Winslow, who was giving a history lesson. Beyond this, they stopped by a great oak beam that ran right down the middle of the cabin, from one side of the ship to the other.

"This is the transverse beam . . . and here is the evidence that bears out my worst fears. For look, a crack begins here, and the wood has already begun to bow, which is why its shifting displaced the deck boards last night, and let in so much water. Put your ear to the wood, Mr Brewster, and tell me what you hear." William Brewster did as he was told.

"I hear a great groaning and a grinding."

"Indeed, you do, for the timbers are no longer tight to the bulwarks. If we were to face another tempest such as we endured last night, that weakness would destroy us. The *Mayflower* would crack asunder, like a nut, and since we are half-way across the great ocean, not a soul would survive."

"Then what is to be done, Master Jones?"

"If the beam were smaller, Mr Bird could remedy the problem by 'fishing' the timber – that is, by attaching further planks to brace and support the beam, and binding it as one might bind a wound. But this is not possible with so large a beam. The seriousness of this injury leads me to believe that we must turn back."

"Turn back? How can we turn back?" Brewster replied with horror, his face grey in the dimness.

"We have no choice, sir. As you see, without restraint this great beam could bend further. It is already out of true, and we have no means to correct it. The beam must be raised and straightened and supported, and it is solid oak and very weighty. No man can raise it and fix it while we are still at sea. It cannot be done. It is impossible. I would have vouched for the safety of the ship below water, but this . . . this is a very serious matter."

"Mr Bird, surely you can do something?" asked Brewster, turning to the ship's carpenter in despair.

"Indeed, sir, no, I cannot. It is the great size of this beam that makes it so difficult to repair. I would need a winch to raise it, so as to lift it high enough for a firm support to be set beneath it, and I would need to apply other measures to counter the buckling of the timber. We have no such device on board. We cannot question the wisdom of our Captain in this matter. We have no choice, but to turn back."

There was a moment's quiet while the men stood pensively in the cabin, listening to the ship's timbers creaking and the voices of the children chanting the names of the Kings of England. Then William Brewster spoke:

"The Lord does not fail His faithful in their hour of need. We sang words of thanks to Him not more than an hour ago. He will not turn against those that have opened their hearts with praise for Him and for His mercy today. That is not the way of the Lord."

"Mr Brewster, even you cannot work miracles. This great beam will continue to twist, and the unsupported timbers around it will snap like twigs in the next tempest, if we cannot reinforce it. We cannot ignore it and endanger the lives of all the good people on board."

"I agree, Mr Jones, but I am a man of faith. For me there will always be a God-given solution to every difficulty, so long as we have faith. Therefore I must ask you to come down with me to the hold, where we may find the answer to your problem. Please follow me, good sirs."

Within minutes, they had descended to the bowels of the ship. Bending low in the darkness beneath the low beams, their scarves held over their mouths to reduce the smell of ballast and other less pleasant things, they fumbled their way along in the gloom. Brewster crept ahead purposefully, with a lantern held in front of him. After a good fifteen minutes of burrowing through piles of boxes, and heaving aside various barrels, the

Pilgrims' leader appeared to have found what he was looking for.

"I brought this with me from Leiden. It is one of the tools of my trade, and I am hopeful . . . as ever . . . that it may do you valuable service. Perhaps, Mr Bird, you could help me open this."

The packing case had been well sealed, and William Bird had to prise the sides open with a jemmy. As the crate dropped open, a rat scampered into the darkness.

William Brewster held a lantern aloft to enable the Captain and his carpenter to see. Christopher Jones gasped in surprise, and moved his lantern closer in order to get a better view. Inside the crate was a large frame, which held in place a metal platen, surmounted by a great vertical screw.

"What engine is this?" asked Richard Bird, in utter amazement.

"It is a device for printing books, good sirs. As you see, it is strong, and has been forged from iron and what I want to know is, will it be strong enough to lift your great beam so that Mr Bird may make his repairs?"

"Possibly . . . Well, yes, indeed. It is not exactly what I had in mind, but it certainly looks as though it might serve... if it is as strong as it looks," observed the carpenter. Captain Jones started to smile, and then gave a low chuckle.

"Clearly we are destined to reach our God-given destination come hell or high water . . ." He hastily added, " Forgive me, Mr Brewster, I spoke only in jest."

"I most certainly hope you did," replied Elder Brewster, thoughtfully.

Captain Jones withdrew to discuss the shifting of the great transverse beam with his principal crew members, Robert Coppin, John Clarke and John Parker. Elder Brewster also talked to the rest of the Brethren. The great iron screw from the press was successfully used to raise the beam and return it to its rightful position and Mr Bird then braced it with further timbers. With the full agreement of the crew and passengers, they continued on their journey.

And so the shifting of the *Mayflower*'s transverse beam was righted in a most unexpected but effective way.

Chapter
9   SAINTS AND SINNERS AT SEA

With the onset of autumn the days grew shorter and colder and the passengers kept below decks as much as they could. The sheer numbers of bodies, so closely crowded, kept the cabin temperature bearable but the nights were chilly. Even though the decks had been freshly caulked, water continued to seep into the sleeping and living quarters. It was safer and warmer to remain indoors, but sometimes it was necessary to visit the upper decks.

The ship's crew were a law unto themselves. They seemed to have no fear as they moved around the ship, whether they were on deck or high in the rigging. Familiarity and experience gave them a spectacular agility that constantly amazed the passengers, who continued to slip and stagger about, hanging on to every rail or rope they could lay hands on to steady themselves. It was usually the servants who had to brave the elements in bad weather. They had to empty chamber-pots and fetch and carry food, water and other items for their masters and their families. They also carried messages between the captain and his mates and the passengers. It could be quite dangerous for those without experienced sea-legs to attempt to walk across the wet, slippery upper decks when the weather was wild.

One November morning, when the sun had just risen, and the sea was particularly rough, John Howland, Deacon Carver's manservant, was staggering along the deck when a massive wave washed him overboard. Like most of the passengers, he didn't know how to swim. Gasping for breath he was pulled down into the turbulence, yelling and screaming for help before he gulped down a mouthful of freezing salt water, and no sooner had he risen to the surface again, than he was plunged once more into the Atlantic. As a wave threw him up for the third time, he saw amidst the froth and foam a loose rope, and with enormous effort threw himself at it and hung on for dear life, shouting like a madman.

As luck would have it, his struggles and cries had been seen and heard by two sailors. They edged their way towards the main-rail head, realising that Howland was hanging on to the topsail-halyards and was being dragged towards the front of the ship where he risked being battered to death, if he did not drown. With speed and a certain amount of risk to themselves, they lowered a rope which Howland managed to pull over his head and under his arms. Then they hauled him in, bruised, frozen and bloody, but very much alive.

Back on ship there was much rejoicing on all sides, particularly from John and Katherine Carver and from Howland's fellow servants, Roger and William. Howland was put to bed straight away in dry clothes and wrapped in a blanket.

Anxious that his servant might have been badly hurt, John Carver asked Giles Heale, the ship's physician and surgeon to pay Howland a visit. During his misadventure, he had been grazed from head to toe, and had lost quite a lot of blood from a deep gash in his arm. Heale examined him carefully, bandaged the arm and gave him a potion to drink which warmed him through.

"You are a very lucky young fellow," observed the ship's doctor, adding,

"... there are others on this ship that are less fortunate than you today."

"And who might those be?" asked Howland, already sleepy from the draft.

"William Button, Mr Fuller's manservant is mortally ill, I fear, and will not see out the week, and Thomas North, a member of the crew, passed away just two hours hence." Yawning widely, John Howland murmured,

"Poor William, he is a gentle fellow. He has a sad disposition, and I think he was hoping that he might regain his health in a new country. May God bless him." Howland also knew Thomas North, but found it difficult to say anything pleasant about him. He had seen him taunt and curse his mistress, Katherine Carver and the young servant girl, Desire Minter, when they had both been seasick. He had disliked North intensely.

Having gained a reputation for baiting and swearing at the passengers, Thomas North had made no friends aboard the *Mayflower*. Captain Jones read a prayer and his body was lowered overboard without further ceremony. It was the first death on the ship. For a man whose favourite joke was that he would throw a sickly passenger off the ship and get to keep their possessions, there was a strange irony in his early death. The sailors saw his passing as an omen, but the Pilgrims saw it as the hand of God at work, and believed that his cruelty and curses had brought about his undoing.

Tumultuous seas for a further five days on end meant that Captain Jones could not hoist the sails – the forces of wind and sea were too strong and totally unpredictable. Nevertheless he continued to steer as direct a course as he could. He was constantly on the move between the helmsman and whipstaff in the steerage cabin, the binnacle (compass) and his own cabin. Night and day he would meticulously chart the route across the Atlantic with the help of a reliable, well-used array of instruments – astrolabe, log line and sand-glass, parallel rulers and dividers. Some nights, he would barely sleep more than two or three hours.

In other parts of the ship the crew and passengers had other concerns. In the galley the ship's cook had long given up serving hot food. The weather was too bad to light a fire and even when it was better, firewood was now in short supply. Hot food was only possible when the sea was

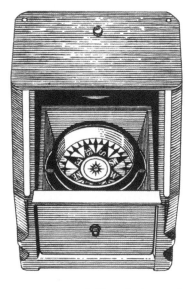

A Binnacle (compass)

calm. The voyagers' diet was fairly monotonous – salted beef and pork (which was sometimes soaked before eating), salted fish of various kinds, oatmeal, peas, cheese, butter, prunes, pickles, raisins and ship's biscuits. Halfway through the voyage, the ship's biscuits provided sustenance and a home for both maggots and weevils. The cook got rid of the maggots in the biscuits by putting a dead fish on top of the sack. The maggots would crawl into the fish and they could be thrown out together. But as the cook was scrupulous with his rations and did not like the idea of wasting a fish (even in such a good cause), he only resorted to this measure every two weeks or so.

An Astrolabe

Two days after the death of William Button, Elizabeth Hopkins gave birth to a boy – Oceanus. He was a puny little thing, but he had a strong pair of lungs and a head of fine, fluffy brown hair, like his father. Shortly after this the wild weather eased off a good deal. The sails were quickly raised and the *Mayflower* was able to make much better progress, tacking into the prevailing wind, under the eagle eye of Captain Jones and his mates, Clark and Coppin.

On 8 November the Captain caught sight of a flock of unusual sea birds flying south, and thought he spotted a whale in the distance, although in those high seas he could not be entirely sure. He felt fairly certain from the charts and by his own intuition that land was not far off. He and the Pilgrim leaders had decided to aim for the Hudson River, which was judged an appropriate area for landing, but he knew little of this coastline. Although two of his crew had negotiated the Atlantic coast before, they were no help to him. Shortly after the third bell, the news came through that the deep sea lead indicated that they were now sailing in only eighty fathoms of water. Jones was confident that the ship was approaching land.

Sure enough, the next day, soon after the seventh bell, when the sky was filled with the grey pallor of early morning, a loud cry came from the main look-out: "Land Ho! Land Ho!" It was about half an hour before sunrise.

Within minutes, everyone was on deck desperate to get their first glimpse of land. Some were swathed in blankets and most had hats on. They emerged from cabins above and below decks, their children in their arms, rubbing the sleep from their eyes. The air was full of anticipation and the passengers clung eagerly to the rails and each other, peering into the gloom, wondering how the crew had managed to see something that seemed so invisible to them. Then, after a momentary hush, somebody yelled:

"Look — yes! I can see it, over yonder!"

"Quite clearly, further left."

"It is land. We have arrived at last. Praise the Lord!"

"What is it? Hills or mountains? I cannot see clearly."

"It is land, and that's enough for me!"

"At last. May we descend from this ship as soon as possible. I never want to go to sea again."

"Praise be! The good Lord has blessed us this day."

And suddenly everyone was gabbling and babbling with enthusiasm. A few of the Pilgrims even broke into song.

William Bradford stood on the poop deck, his arm round the shoulders of his young wife, Dorothy. They stared at the thin line of land visible on the horizon. The light of the rising sun made the land mass clearer with every second.

"That land will be our new home, Dorothy – for us and our children and theirs after them."

". . . and soon little John will be with us. He will be elder brother to an entire family that will grow up in a good new world, praise the Lord," Dorothy replied. She had shed many tears over the two-year-old son she had left behind in Holland. Her greatest consolation had been looking after the other children on board the ship, caring for them when their parents were not well enough to do so. Whenever help was needed, Dorothy was always the first to offer. She had helped with the delivery of

Oceanus, and had played with little Damaris Hopkins while Elizabeth was nursing her new baby.

The voyagers never forgot the day when they had first sighted land. For many it was a moment of joy and optimism such as they had not experienced during their long confinement on the ship. After more than sixty days of rattling around in the gloom, feeling cold, sick and miserable, the dawn of that day and the hope and expectation they felt seemed to make it all worth while. For many, it was the moment when they believed that their troubles were over. Despite the bitter chill of late autumn, the morning sunshine filled them with excitement and a feeling of expectation — expectation, and the promise of a new start, a new opportunity and a new day.

Soon after they had sighted land, the weather grew worse, and the passengers were driven back to their cabins. A harsh wind began to blow, and the sky alternated between gathering clouds and a deep icy winter blue. There was to be no plain sailing for Captain Jones. The general consensus had been that they should sail southwards towards the Hudson River, but as they approached the land, the water suddenly became much shallower, and they encountered shifting sandy shoals and wild breakers. The elation of the morning gave way to fear, as Christopher Jones realised that he was perilously close to wrecking his ship somewhere off the coast of America, before they had even landed.

With improbable speed and sheer determination, he turned the ship about and steered it out of danger as quickly as he could. Hundreds of orders were given to the crew who sprang into action, understanding the danger they faced. He aimed the *Mayflower* towards Cape Cod, further along the coast, which gave the Pilgrims a chance to see a shoreline of gentle

The *Mayflower's circuitous route to Cape Cod*

hills and deep woods tumbling down to the water's edge.

While Captain Jones had been occupied with the threat posed by those uncharted waters, Elder Brewster, William Bradford, Edward Winslow and John Carver were tackling a very different threat to the safety of their community – from disorder and opportunism amongst the voyagers.

An argumentative group, which included John Billingham and Francis Eaton, were complaining that they had come under a royal patent granted for Virginia, but it did not cover that part of the country where they now seemed likely to settle. This being the case, they reckoned that they owed no allegiance to any authority once they had landed. The Pilgrim leaders became increasingly alarmed by the growing signs of rebellion, and decided that something must be done to ensure that a rule of order and responsibility was maintained. Acting quickly, Brewster, Bradford and Carver hatched a plan to avert social chaos. They drafted a document – the *Mayflower* Compact – that was agreed upon and signed by every male passenger on the ship.

This simple, democratic contract laid the foundation for the

The Signing of the Mayflower *Compact*

constitutional social order upheld by that small community for many years to come. Its construction revealed just how far-sighted and inspired the Pilgrim leaders were. By getting every single adult male on the ship to sign his hand to it, a great deal of potential trouble was averted.

> *In the name of God, Amen. We, whose names are underwritten, the Loyal Subjects of our dread Sovereign lord, King James, by the Grace of God, of England, France and Ireland, King, Defender of the Faith, &c. Having undertaken for the Glory of God, and Advancement of the Christian Faith, and the Honour of our King and Country, a voyage to plant the first colony in the northern parts of Virginia, do by these present, solemnly and mutually in the Presence of God and one of another, covenant and combine ourselves together into a civil body politic, for our better ordering and preservation, and furtherance of the ends aforesaid; And by virtue hereof to enact, constitute, and frame, such just and equal laws, ordinances, acts, constitutions and offices, from time to time, as shall be thought most meet and convenient for the general good of the colony; unto which we promise all due submission and obedience. In Witness whereof we have hereunto subscribed our names at Cape Cod the eleventh of November, in the reign of our sovereign lord, King James of England, France and Ireland, the eighteenth, and of Scotland the fifty-fourth. anno Domini, 1620.*

Chapter

10 THE LANDINGS

No sooner had the anchor been dropped at Cape Cod, then everything changed. The breeze fell and the groaning and creaking of the ship diminished as she swayed gently in the shelter of the calm grey winter waters.

While the men assembled in the 'tween deck cabin to sign the Compact, the crew lowered the sails and tended to the ship. Five women wandered onto the lower deck having left their children in the care of the ever-patient Dorothy Bradford. They looked out longingly at the distant view of hills, trees and the green and brown undulating coastline and wondered how long it would take before they could unpack their belongings and begin their new lives. Susanna Chilton, a pale and gentle soul who had suffered terribly from seasickness, wondered what sort of houses they would build in this land that would be their new home, while Elinor Billington, who had earned a reputation for being tough and forthright, remarked that she would rather know how soon she would be able to wash the family's clothes, a comment that made the other women laugh.

By early afternoon, the Compact had been signed by all of the men fit enough to do so, and soon afterwards the ship's boat was lowered into the water, carrying fifteen men on their first voyage of exploration. The boat returned that evening to the shouts and cheers of family and friends keen to know what they had discovered. The main purpose of this foray had been to gather wood, which was now in short supply. The choice of juniper was particularly popular, since its pungent fragrance offset the sour smell of overcrowded bodies below deck. Also, now that they had fire-wood and the sea was calmer, the ship's cook was able to prepare some warm food for the first time in many weeks.

The explorers described the landscape they had seen: a coastline bordered by a great many kinds of trees – fir, oak, pine, juniper, cedar and sassafras, as well as sweeping sand dunes and some grassland that might be suitable for cultivation.

The next day was Sunday, the day of rest, and the company remained on board. William Brewster's prayers were held on the upper deck and despite a sharp breeze, many passengers, including some of the most feeble, hurried to hear him. It was a pale and sickly congregation that huddled beneath shawls, cloaks and hats to listen to his words of faith and hope. Brewster's fine voice rose above the noise of the ship, the lapping waves and the cries of the sea birds.

"Today is the twelfth of November, and I shall read from the twelfth chapter of Proverbs. The words of the good book speak to us as clearly and truly as if we had asked the Lord a question, and He had answered us:

"He that loveth instruction, loveth knowledge: but he that hateth correction is a fool. A good man getteth favour of the Lord: but the man of wicked imagination will he condemn. A man cannot be established by wickedness: but the root of the righteous shall not be moved."

He paused and looked up at the congregation before him, wondering if the troublemakers that had pushed the Pilgrims into writing the Compact were there, but Billingham and Eaton were conspicuous by their absence.

Monday the 13th of November was set aside for exploration and work. Bradford, Brewster, Carver and Winslow had spent the early hours of the morning in the poop cabin with Captain Jones, poring over maps in the light of a pallid dawn. Jones explained how they had been compelled to drop anchor somewhat further north than he had originally intended. He

The Pilgrims land in the New World

pointed to the map, in the small pool of yellow light thrown by the lantern hanging over his table.

"The shoals and seas decided much for us, as you may see. Nonetheless, this could be a suitable region for exploration and settlement, could it not, gentlemen?"

Elder Brewster replied, "Choosing a place to live and farm for many generations can never be a task lightly undertaken, Master Jones. It is my belief that to find the blessed ground that God intends for us, and that will prove fertile and favourable to us may take some time."

"Time is a gift we do not have," the Captain replied.

"That being the case, how long do we have to search for land suitable for settlement?" asked William Bradford.

"Such a question may seem reasonable to you, but unfortunately it is not. We cannot stay even a day longer than necessary. The ship must return to England as soon as possible to replenish its provisions. Already there is sickness amongst us that shows that we are in need of fresh food. Our provisions were never great. We are all in danger of starvation and that risk increases, the longer my ship stays here. We must move quickly, and decisions must be made quickly."

"Poor decisions made in haste may take years to rectify. This is a lesson I have learnt the hard way," said Brewster.

"Winter is upon us. The weather can only get worse. Here, in your new home you may find food scarce now. But I must return before my crew suffers starvation."

"We will do our best to act promptly," said William Brewster, wearily. The others said nothing.

Later that day, as the long boat slid towards the shore and the men lifted their oars in preparation for landing, William Bradford turned to Deacon Carver:

"Well, brother, we have reached our new home at last, even though there are no friends to welcome us and no inns to shelter us from the night. What dangers lie ahead of us, do you suppose?"

"The dangers I fear are perpetual hunger and cold," replied Carver, lowering his voice and drawing his coat closer to his body, "and our isolation in this unknown land."

Bradford turned and looked back at the little *Mayflower*, bobbing on the water in the bay. Their home for so many months would soon be leaving them behind – alone in a strange country.

Yet the Pilgrims achieved a great deal that day, even though not all of their discoveries were to prove reassuring. When they brought the shallop out onto dry land, ready to reassemble, they made an unwelcome discovery. What with the storms and the pressure of bodies sleeping and sitting in the boat, its components no longer fitted together. The ship's carpenter carefully examined the various pieces on shore, and declared that it would be at least two weeks' work before the boat would be seaworthy. Somewhat reluctantly, Captain Jones agreed to let the Pilgrims use the ship's long boat for their first explorations. Bradford and Brewster thanked him warmly.

Once on land, the women got busy washing the clothes for their families and themselves in the fresh icy water, while a party of sixteen men set out under the captaincy of Miles Standish. Dressed in helmets and corslets and armed with match-lock muskets and swords, they carried minimal provisions.

This was the moment that Standish had been waiting for. He knew that when the Pilgrims reached land he would have an important role to play. As their military leader, his task was to lead the men against any unexpected foes and unknown dangers that they might encounter. Small and fiery-tempered, he would later show himself a just and compassionate man. Pastor John Robinson had met Standish in Leiden and trusted him immediately. The army captain had worked his way up from the ranks, starting out as a drummer boy and later serving in the English army in Holland, fighting for the Dutch against Spain. He was sympathetic to the Separatists, but never considered himself to be one of their brotherhood.

It was his task to lead that first foray into unknown territory. The party set out walking in single file, following the coastline. They hadn't gone much more than a mile when they saw the first sign of human life –

'The women got busy washing the clothes for their families'

five or six people, evidently Native Americans, with a dog. But as soon as the Indians caught a glimpse of the strangers, they whistled up their dog and ran off, leaving the explorers following them inland, slowly but determinedly. Soon the pursuers were left far behind, tramping heavily through a dank and wintry forest. They tracked the Indians' footsteps for a further ten miles before the light began to fade and Standish decided to pitch camp. Three of the group kept watch while the others gathered wood, lit a fire, talked and slept.

Next morning, as soon as the light was good enough, they set about following the Indians' tracks again until they reached a long river creek. From this point they made better progress for a while, marching as quickly as their armour permitted, trekking into another wood, where they found no further signs of life. Here the path was very rough, and they slowed down again. They marched on without speaking but the ringing of their corslets and their heavy footfalls startled small flocks of birds and deer as they tramped up hill and down dale. The bushes and shrubs became increasingly thick and they soon lost sight of any kind of path. Forcing their way through the dense undergrowth, they tore and scratched their clothes and themselves. Worse still, they were growing desperately thirsty. They had taken minimal provisions when they set out – dry biscuits, cheese and a little bottle of aqua-vitae.

By mid-morning they had reached a deep valley full of shrubs, bushes and long grass, thankfully with some visible paths running through it. They saw deer and at last found some springs of fresh water. This was the first New England water they had tasted, and they drank slowly and deeply, thanking God again and again for this much-needed refreshment. Miles Standish now decided to change direction and march south in order to get back to the shore. Conscious that their friends on ship might be growing anxious for their safety, they signalled their position by lighting a fire.

They set off again, trudging several miles towards the coast, but Standish could see that some of the party were beginning to flag. Some were now so far behind that he was afraid they might get lost in the dense and darkening forest. They regrouped and he re-directed the party inland, so that they could walk on the sand beside the river, an altogether easier surface for the tired, footsore company. His decision to turn inland when he did was more than just lucky – it probably saved many of them from starvation and early death. Divine providence, it seemed, was guiding their footsteps. Their path took them towards a number of curious sand heaps, some covered in mats and others with various apparently random objects on them, including an earthenware pot, a bow and some arrows. Looking more closely, they decided that they had probably come to a burial ground, and moved on.

Their next discovery was to prove crucial: it looked like the remains of a dwelling of some kind, and inside they found a large ship's kettle. Beside it was another sand mound, and, scrabbling beneath the surface, they uncovered some huge baskets of Indian corn, so big that it took two of them to carry one. They took as many of these as they could carry and they also filled up the kettle with corn and took that as well, promising themselves that when the shallop was in working order, they would return and leave payment for their find. The rest of the corn they pushed into their pockets or reburied. They named this place Cornhill.

Trudging on, they came upon an old fort and a fence and as they walked back along the river, two canoes. That night they pitched camp near the fresh water pond they had discovered earlier. At this point the weather started to change for the worse, and though they built a great fire to keep warm, the rain poured down all night. Next morning they traipsed down to the shore with their heavy baskets, weary, hungry and soaked through. There they fired off their guns by way of greeting and Captain Jones lowered the long boat and brought the explorers back to the *Mayflower*. Exhausted but elated by their adventures, they gathered that

Indian corn

evening in groups, drinking beer and warming themselves, recounting what had happened and what they had found.

Yet reaching land brought its own particular trials and dangers. While the exploration party had been marching through the harsh countryside, the others had been busy looking for wood and sawing up timber to mend the shallop, but their progress had been slow because they were desperately cold. Except at high tide, the only way they could reach the shore was by wading from the long boat, sometimes thigh deep in freezing water. Their clothes were soaked through and they never had an opportunity to dry off as they shivered and worked through the short winter days.

No matter how committed they were to the success of the expedition, the combination of the poor shipboard diet and unhygienic

The Old Fort and Meeting House

living conditions, and now their exposure to chill winds in wet and freezing clothes all conspired to undermine their health. It was scarcely surprising that an infectious disease, which may have started as no more than a cold or a virus, was taking a hold of them and gradually spreading through their little community.

As soon as the shallop had been rebuilt, plans got underway for a second expedition, this time involving some thirty-four men, ten of them sailors. As a gesture of trust, the Pilgrim leaders had decided to invite Captain Jones to lead this excursion. Part of the team set out on foot, while others used the shallop. This time, however, things started to go wrong almost immediately. Within hours of leaving the ship, a terrible storm blew up and the shallow boat was soon water-logged and forced to land at the first opportunity.

Meanwhile the party on foot, marching some six or seven miles ahead of the boat, were buffeting their way through the same storm. Bitter winter gusts whipped round them and snow fell for the rest of that day and into the night. The land beneath their feet and the clothes they wore were now freezing. Even the best and bravest struggled to keep their spirits up.

Next day, the snowstorm slackened off, and the group with the shallop reboarded and sailed up the Pamet River, the creek they had discovered on their first foray. They landed and marched along the bank for about five miles until night fell, when they pitched camp. They had intended to follow the river but the ground was too rough, so they returned to the place where they had found the corn. This time they made a number of further discoveries – a bottle of oil and several more corn heaps, as well as mounds of beans. But by now the ground was frozen and covered with snow, so that if they had not found the stores of food on their earlier expedition, they would never have discovered them at all. They would have starved and there would have been no corn for them to plant in the following spring. Their trust in God's providence had been rewarded, and would continue to be rewarded again and again.

The Shallop

PART 3

New World

Chapter

11 DANGERS BY LAND AND SEA

M any of the Pilgrims wanted to settle down in Cape Cod as quickly as possible. They were finding life at sea increasingly unbearable – the sour smell of stale bodies, the damp, cold and wet and the discomfort of living in such airless, crowded and cramped conditions. But William Bradford and Edward Winslow were not convinced that they had found the best place to establish the colony. William Brewster was unable to offer them any advice. As their Elder, and one of the older passengers, it was considered inappropriate for him to trudge round the countryside with a musket. Without having seen it or what it had to offer he was unable to offer an opinion.

At first glance, there was much to recommend the place. The fishing seemed excellent. Many whales had been sighted which might have provided them with a valuable source of meat, bone and oil. Unafraid of the *Mayflower*, one large whale had inspected the tiny ship and chosen to bask beside it in the winter sun. She floated about thirty yards off, puffing out a great spout of water from time to time. One intrepid soul loaded his musket and took aim, whereupon it exploded in its entirety, lock, stock and barrel. Luckily nobody was hurt, but the message was clear to the great beast, which slowly slid beneath the icy Atlantic waters, depriving them of another chance.

Fed up with being cooped-up on shipboard for months, the children were becoming increasingly impatient and fractious. On the fifth day after arriving at Cape Cod their boredom revealed itself all too clearly when a lethal game came close to finishing them all off. Francis Billingham, the fourteen-year-old son of the troublemaker John Billingham had been tinkering with his father's gun, as well as making squibs out of gunpowder. He decided to test the firearm on some canvases draped across the 'tween decks cabin, and with a dreadful bang and billows of choking black smoke, came dangerously close to causing a serious fire. Both father and son were strongly reprimanded. Several people thought that both parties deserved a good whipping for exposing them all to such unnecessary danger.

Incidents such as this, and the voyagers' rapidly declining strength and health were beginning to erode the relationship between the passengers and the crew, who were getting more and more impatient to get back to England.

Squabbles broke out between passengers and sailors over trivial problems – rations, safety, children occupying decks when repairs were in progress and conduct in general. Some of the women were afraid of the crew, but they were equally apprehensive about their husbands going on exploratory expeditions. Dorothy Bradford was particularly anxious, but did not wish to complain, realising that it was necessary for her husband to make reconnaissance trips as often as possible. She was prone to dissolve into tears, which she attributed to missing her little son. Each expedition caused her fearful anxiety about the safety of her husband and at times she wept inconsolably.

William tried to distract his young wife's attention by talking about their adventures. He described in detail how they had made a number of strange and exciting discoveries. They had dug up the skeletons of a man and a child which had been embalmed in some kind of strange red powder. The child had been adorned with beads and a small bow. The expedition party had carefully removed some of the prettier and more valuable items from the grave. But while William recounted all this, Dorothy grew even more upset:

"Surely these people will be angry if their places of burial have been disturbed?" she asked. William confidently assured her that the Indians would never detect any changes to their burial mounds.

"But what of all those pots and baskets and dishes that you brought back with you? They will surely miss them, will they not?"

"We will pay for those when we return."

"But perhaps by then it will be too late. Perhaps they already believe that we have stolen from them. What weapons do these people use?"

"Spears, bows and arrows, I believe."

"Oh, William you must take care. We may already have given the people of this land very good reason to hate and fear us. I have a feeling that you have displeased them by disturbing their places of rest. When you go out tomorrow, you must be extra vigilant. Promise me you will pay special attention to unexpected dangers."

"It is not good to be so fearful, Dorothy. You must have faith in the Lord, who loves and cares for us at all times. He will protect us, you may be sure," William replied reassuringly. But Dorothy was filled with an inexplicable apprehension for her husband and the expedition next morning.

Bradford left her and went up to the great cabin to meet the Captain and Brewster, Standish, Carver and Winslow, who were busy discussing whether or not the community should settle in Cape Cod.

"Some of the men feel that Cornhill may be the best choice for a colony as it provides a reliable harbour for boats," observed Miles Standish. "I am told that it does not accommodate ships," said William Brewster.

"This is true, but it must be said that Cornhill is still my choice. In my opinion, we cannot expect our men to explore too many miles of a terrain that they do not know," said John Carver. "Every day we all become weaker. We must make a decision soon."

"If it were my choice, you would choose Cornhill and build your homes there and be done with. Then the ship would be able to hoist sails forthwith," growled Captain Jones. The others continued their discussion, preferring to ignore the Captain's remark.

"There is a group, and I believe them to be well informed, that say that Agawan, to the north of this place, is altogether better," pointed out Edward Winslow, adding, "It cannot be said that there is a great deal of water at Cornhill. My view is that a third expedition is imperative if we are to find the best place to set up a colony that will serve us long and well."

"Brother Edward is right," said William Bradford. "I propose that we look further before we decide, even though some of us are weak. We cannot afford to make a mistake. It would be terrible if we were left to fend for ourselves in a place that failed to provide us with adequate ground to till or draw water, or indeed proved unsafe in other ways."

And so a group of twenty men was selected for a third expedition. They set out on December 6, determined to explore the bay opposite Cape Cod. Their aim was to establish if there was a good harbour there.

The weather was bad and getting worse. A winter storm had been blowing for several days. Flakes of snow would land on the ship from time to time and the children would run out to see how much of the white slush was to be found on the upper decks. Although the *Mayflower* was well and truly anchored (she had five), the violent seas could still rock her about in harbour.

Filled with a sudden restlessness, Dorothy Bradford put on a hat and scarf and wandered out onto the upper deck. It was chilly and the ship was bobbing up and down on a choppy sea. As Dorothy peered through the fine sleet and snow, she was horrified to see three young children playing on the forecastle. One of them was hanging on the rigging, swinging backwards and forwards in the wind. Another child, a toddler, was precariously balanced on the rigging rail on the outer side of the adventure.

Dorothy ran across the deck towards the foremast and beyond, and did not stop until she had seized the hand of one of the children, Joseph Mullins, and pulled him onto the upper deck. Another child, John Tinker, had climbed over the rail unaided, but little Damaris Hopkins, who was barely two years old, was still teetering on the rail, having apparently followed the older children on their precarious venture.

Dorothy climbed over the railing, and clutching the shroud with her left hand, lifted the small child to safety over the railing. At that moment the ship gave a sudden and unexpected lurch. A powerful wave had struck the *Mayflower* broadside on, and her feet slipped from under her. For a second or two she hung onto the shroud rope with one hand, but her petticoat had become entangled on a nail, which was ripping into her skirt. With her other hand she sought to release the fabric from the nail, but as she did so the ship heaved again and she fell backwards.

The children on the forecastle screamed, and two of the crew hurried over to see the young woman upside-down, held only by the lace on her petticoat, caught on the nail. As the third wave struck, there was a ripping sound and Dorothy fell backwards into the water, her mouth open in a cry for help, into the icy Atlantic waves. Within a few moments, she had been knocked unconscious against the side of the ship. Her clothing was now saturated with water and this, combined with the powerful winter currents surging around the *Mayflower*, dragged her body under.

The children watched in helpless horror as did the sailors. It was all over in a matter of minutes, and they knew only too well that it was impossible for anyone to survive in that icy sea. Little Damaris screamed and screamed, but by the time they had lowered the boat and pulled Dorothy's body out of the sea, she was dead.

Three days later, in the evening, as the sun had almost disappeared behind the hills, the expedition returned in the shallop. Bradford, like the others of the party, was full of news of the extraordinary and frightening adventures they had encountered and the discoveries they had made. He was longing to see his young wife and tell her everything.

It fell to Elder Brewster to give William the terrible news. They sat and talked for hour after hour; two men, like father and son, going over the tragedy and the strange way it had unfolded. They both knew that the loss of her life was God's will. They accepted this without question.

In the morning they were still together. Elder Brewster drew his protégé to his side, and they opened the great bible together. With scrupulous care and respect the older man turned the pages of the leather-bound book, alighting almost by chance on a passage towards the end of the volume.

Brewster held the lantern over the text, which had opened on a page entitled 'The Holy Gospel of Jesus Christ, according to Matthew'. It was a favourite page for many of the Pilgrims and their children. Opposite the opening words of the gospel was a decorative map with little pictures of castles, churches and mountains, and in the sea were sailing ships and several

The defcription of the holie land and of the places mencioned in the foure Euangeliftes.

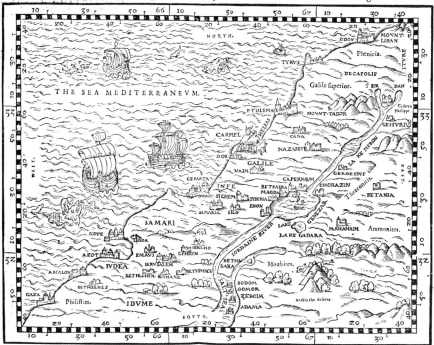

The Holy Gospel of Jesus Christ, according to Matthew from the Geneva Bible

strange sea beasts. The map was called 'The description of the holy land and of the places mentioned in the four Evangelists'. William Bradford had seen this page many times. It felt as familiar as an old friend.

Brewster turned the pages and alighted on Chapter Five, under the title 'The Blessed'. In a quiet voice he started to read the words spoken by Jesus Christ to his disciples on the mountain:

> *Blessed are the poor in spirit, for theirs is the kingdom of heaven.*
>
> *Blessed are they that mourn: for they shall be comforted.*
>
> *Blessed are the meek: for they shall inherit the earth.*
>
> *Blessed are they which hunger and thirst for righteousness:*
> *for they shall be filled.*
>
> *Blessed are the merciful: for they shall obtain mercy.*
>
> *Blessed are the pure in heart: for they shall see God.*
>
> *Blessed are the peace makers: for they shall be called the children of God.*
>
> *Blessed are they that suffer persecution for righteousness sake:*
> *for theirs is the kingdom of heaven.*

Chapter

12 PLYMOUTH OR PATUXET?

The twenty men chosen for the third expedition included Miles Standish, John Carver, William Bradford, Edward Winslow, John Tilley, Edward Tilley and John Howland. There were also some members of the crew, including two of the Captain's mates – Master Clarke and Master Coppin and the master gunner. They set off in the shallop, and hadn't gone far when William Bradford and Edward Winslow saw that two of the men were far from well – Edward Tilley had a terrible cold and a hacking cough and the gunner was white and sweating. But it was too late to go back.

First of all they sailed out to the bay opposite Cape Cod, as they had planned. The weather was freezing and they didn't have the right clothes for the icy New England winter at its worst. More than once their coats became as rigid as cardboard in the cold air, and the hair on their heads and faces froze. A bitter wind filled the sail and kept the boat moving, and they sailed for some six or seven leagues (30 kilometres or more) along the coast.

Drawing closer to the beach they spotted a party of about ten Indians standing over something, but as soon as they caught sight of the Pilgrims they ran off. The expedition pulled into the shore and camped there for the night. The next day they divided: eight were to stay on the boat and the rest ventured inland to see what could be found. They had heard that there was a harbour and river near this part of the coast, but so far they had found nothing that fitted that description. They discovered a dead dolphin on the beach, which they called a grampus, naming that place

102

Grampus Bay. Now they realised that it must have been a dolphin that the Indians had been examining because there were quite a few lying dead on the shore; but although they were known to be a rich source of oil, the exploration party had more urgent tasks to attend to.

They came to the place where they had seen the Indians, and followed them, tracking them into the woods. At around this point, the party on foot lost sight of the shallop, but continued as best they could, through the trees and shrub-land. They made various discoveries, finding fields where corn had been sown in previous years, and they also discovered an Indian burial ground surrounded by a wooden fence. The burial mounds were lovingly decorated with finely-wrought wreaths and boughs. As the snow fell, William Bradford and Edward Winslow found themselves staring at that desolate spot, silent and thoughtful.

"I know not why, but it reminds me of the churchyard at Scrooby," said William Bradford.

"It is a pagan place, yet it is holy for those whose loved ones are buried here," replied his friend. They did not cross the threshold.

Some miles further on, they found several Indian houses, but they seemed abandoned. Slowly the sun sank in the darkling sky, and they emerged from the woods to see the shallop moored at some distance away. With much hooting and yelling, they succeeded in attracting the attention of their friends on the boat. Then they pitched camp for the night.

Hungry, cold and tired, even the effort of pitching camp was almost more than some of them could bear. They had to find enough firewood, and prepare the small quantity of food they had brought with them. They were extremely hungry, having eaten nothing that day.

Several hours later, towards midnight they were woken by the sentry shouting:

"Arm! Arm! Wake up! Arm yourselves!"

Out of the darkness came an unearthly cry that filled them with terror and apprehension. They fired off a couple of musket rounds, and waited.

"It must be foxes or wolves," whispered Edward Winslow to Bradford.

Round the campfire

"I hope so, but I have never heard them make such a noise," returned his friend.

"That is because they are foreign beasts, and do not speak our language," replied Edward cheerfully.

They awoke stiff and tired next morning, several hours before the sun was up. They fed the fire, and a couple of men started to inspect their muskets. They were anxious that, what with the wet and the cold, their firearms were not working properly, so by way of a test they fired off a couple of rounds. They echoed strangely in that wintry silence.

Then, in the cold early morning gloom, the Pilgrims knelt in a circle and prayed together. They asked God to give them the strength and determination they needed to find the spot where they should live, which would serve them well and become their home, theirs and their children's. The morning prayers greatly strengthened their resolve. John Howland and one of the crew members then prepared the breakfast, while the others decided to carry their heavy armour down to the shallop. Others were afraid of leaving themselves vulnerable, and felt that they should be prepared for any unexpected dangers that might suddenly loom out of the dark winter woodland. Their fears were soon justified.

As they were quietly busying themselves about the camp, one and then another of the strange cries rang out from the trees. This time there could be no doubt – they were not the cries of any wild beast. One of the Pilgrims shouted:

"Look out! They're attacking us!" Panic ensued and it seemed as though everyone was screaming at once. Arrows rained down on them, yet somehow, unbelievably, no one was hurt.

"Where are the men with the arms and belongings?" hissed Bradford, as he ducked his head down.

"Some are here, and the rest are making for the shallop," replied Master Clarke. Men were running everywhere, dodging arrows and searching for their muskets. Miles Standish fired off his flint-lock musket, which made a tremendous noise. Moments later, he followed it up with a second shot.

"Get down and don't fire unless you can take aim," he sang out. The men did as he bade.

Peering out from under a bush, Bradford could now see one particularly tall man behind an oak tree priming his bow, ready to take aim. "Brother John," he shouted. "Look yonder, the leader is behind that oak tree." John Carver fired his musket and with a strange whoop, the leader of the group ran off. They listened, with relief, to the soft patter of feet hurrying away in the gloom of the early morning.

Though they did not realise it, the Pilgrims were invading the land of the Wampanoags, or people from the East, an ancient and spiritual community. Twenty years earlier, there had been perhaps 12,000 of them living in tranquillity, planting their corn and hunting. By the time the *Mayflower* arrived, the population had been reduced to less than half that number. This was why the Pilgrims had found so many burial grounds.

For the Wampanoags, the white men brought death. It wasn't merely the cruelty of the earliest colonists, though they had taken a number of them prisoner, with a view to selling them as slaves to the Spanish. It was their 'invisible bullets', the bacteria and viruses that the Europeans carried with them that decimated the Wampanoags, who had no immunity against these unfamiliar diseases. Five major epidemics had swept across the east coast of America in the five years before the *Mayflower* arrived, and in one place, Patuxet, the entire population had died. No wonder the Wampanoags tried to drive them away: the white men brought sickness, slavery and death.

A Pilgrim ready for action

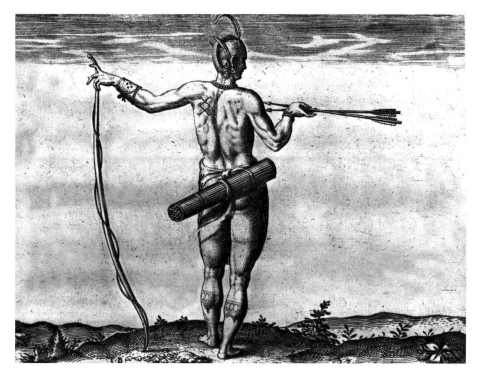

Native American warrior

The Pilgrims knew nothing of this history of persecution as bitter as their own. To them, the Indians were their attackers, infidels who must be tamed or appeased. Yet they were less brutal than the colonists who preceded them. Their love for Jesus made them prefer peace and negotiation above aggression and the use of arms. But they feared and were feared by the Wampanoags, and fear makes people cruel.

After the attack, the expedition split up: one group was to follow their mysterious attackers, and the other to guard the shallop. From time to time each group would call to the other and fire a musket to frighten off enemies. But after they had followed them a short distance, Captain Standish ordered them to return.

They duly thanked God that not a single soul had been hurt, although some coats hung over the camp barricade were now full of holes, made by Indian arrows. They never found out precisely how many men there were in that raiding party but the general consensus was that it must have been about thirty. They named that place in the dripping woods, 'The First Encounter.'

Elated by God's generosity and mercy in protecting them, they set off in the shallop in high spirits, with a fair wind behind them, and sailed further up the coast, continuing their search for a river or creek.

After about two hours it began to sleet and snow, and the breeze started to pick up. Soon the sea became very choppy and while they were struggling painfully to hold a steady course in the wind and waves, the hinges of the rudder suddenly snapped, making it almost impossible to steer. Undeterred, they tried to keep the boat on course with the help of the oars, but the sea was growing increasingly rough, and the short hours of daylight were drawing to a close. As darkness fell some of them began to lose heart and hope. Suddenly Robert Coppin yelled out:

"Harbour in sight! Harbour in sight! Be of good cheer, sailors!"

By now a strong gale was blowing and without a rudder they were dependent on the shallop's sail to carry them where they wanted to go. Navigating as best they could, they made their way towards this newly-discovered harbour. But a series of icy waves struck the boat amidships, and the patched-up mast suddenly split into three pieces.

"What is to be done now, Master Coppin?" shouted Miles Standish, above the deafening storm.

"Should we abandon the boat?" asked John Carver.

"I think not, Mr Carver. We must hope the tide is with us, and if that is the case, all is not lost," replied Coppin, at the top of his voice. And once again, though they did not realise it at the time, they were blessed by more than good luck. The tide was indeed with them, but what was even more extraordinary – if they had been able to steer the course northward that Master Coppin had recommended, they would probably have been thrown onto the rocks, and wrecked. Almost without thinking, John Carver found himself murmuring the words of John the Apostle, "*The wind bloweth where it listeth*", as wind and tide carried the shallop, without sail or rudder, onto a sand bank.

They had landed on the leeward side of a small island, where they stayed and rested from the howling wind and rain, while keeping a sharp look-out for unexpected dangers. The next morning they set out to discover where they were, and found that the place was uninhabited. The following day was Sunday, the day of rest and prayer.

On Monday, 21st of December, 1620, having repaired the shallop as best they could, they sailed into the bay, and landed on Plymouth Rock. They did not yet know that the famous adventurer, Captain John Smith, had already named that site 'Plymouth'. Later, they adopted that name themselves, either out of respect for his choice, or in memory of their last sight of the old world. But the Wampanoags had their own name for that place: they called it Patuxet.

This was the spot they had been looking for. The harbour was larger than that at Cape Cod, and there were cornfields with good soil that had been planted and tilled until recently, and brooks with clean, clear running water. There were woods nearby with a great variety of trees, both familiar and unfamiliar. At last it seemed as if all their patience had been rewarded. They returned to the shallop as quickly as they could, and rowed back to the *Mayflower* and their wives, friends and families, full of the news of their adventures and discoveries. But for William Bradford, returning in high spirits with the others, there awaited the news of Dorothy's death.

Captain John Smith

Bradford preferred not to talk of his loss to anyone, apart from William Brewster. Elder Brewster had a wisdom that no other man shared on that ship. He alone could explain how the God that had taken Dorothy's life was the same God that had protected Bradford and the rest during their days of adventure and exploration. The Lord to whom Bradford prayed so fervently every day had decided to take Dorothy back to Him. If he could learn to accept and understand this as God's will, he would become a better man, he knew. But he also knew that God would understood it if he mourned her death inwardly, as he did day after day and night after night, whenever he was alone.

After due consultation between the exploration team and its leaders, Captain Jones and his crew weighed anchor and the cry went up "Make Sail! Make Sail!" A wave of new-found hope and optimism ran through the ship, and for a moment even the sun managed to break through the heavy clouds. But then the bad weather returned, and once more they had to be patient before they could regain the Rock, and their new home.

The moment of their arrival was greeted with quiet excitement. At the first opportunity, they lowered the long boat (the shallop was now in need of drastic repairs), and made their way onto land. Everything about the bay seemed right. They had seen many fish, including shell fish, and all sorts of birds as well. Long discussions now ensued about the exact spot on which to establish the colony – among the possibilities was a site three miles inland, up a creek, and also a small island, but the first was too far from the fishing grounds and too near the woods where they had been attacked, while the second was too bleak and wooded, and the fresh water supply was uncertain.

Eventually the Pilgrims agreed upon the mainland. Careful inspection showed that there was a piece of high ground where fresh water was easily accessible, with an area that had already been cleared for the cultivation of corn. It was close to a deep natural harbour which could serve boats and ships of all sizes. A small hill close by gave an excellent view on all sides, including out to sea, and seemed the ideal spot for a fort.

No sooner had they made their choice than they set about building. The first structure to go up was the Common House, or storehouse, which had to be strong enough to contain their dwindling provisions and arms, and large enough to serve as a hospital and church as well.

Although every day brought new opportunities, they were fighting against the harsh New England winter and their own failing health. More and more of the voyagers had fallen ill, particularly the women. Perhaps it was so many days spent indoors in the close atmosphere of the *Mayflower's* cabins, with constant exposure to each others' germs, that contributed to the spread of a chest infection that now affected almost all of them, to a greater or lesser degree. Or perhaps the women had passed on so much of their food to their children that they had less resistance to the illness.

The building itself was slow, laborious and labour-intensive. Trees had to be felled, and then sawn up, and carried for more than two hundred yards to the construction site, and most days the driving wind, snow, sleet and rain made their task desperately difficult. When the gales were at their worst, it became impossible to leave the ship. On Christmas day, they drank a little beer, thanks to the kindness of Captain Jones, otherwise they would have had to celebrate with water, biscuits and dried meat. But despite the bitter cold, the shortage of food and their poor health, their hope and faith remained indomitable.

Chapter

13 FEAR AND FRIENDSHIP

S hortly after the completion of the Common House, William Bradford fell ill. He had thrown himself into the business of planning and building as energetically as he could and had achieved a great deal. But he had a racking cough and a sense of great weariness and cold within. Everything became vague and dreamlike, and then he remembered nothing.

He awoke to find himself lying on a straw mattress in a room he did not recognise. Hot, weak and confused, he tried to work out where he was, peering towards the dim light of an open doorway. Light was also coming in from two small windows that appeared to be covered in waxed paper. On the far side of the room were benches and shuttered windows. In the distance he could hear the familiar sound of hammering and the rhythmic squeak of a saw.

For a moment he thought that Dorothy was walking towards him, pretty and round, as he remembered her from the old days, before the three months on board the *Mayflower* had taken their toll. But as she drew closer, he saw that it was not Dorothy but the motherly shape of Mary Brewster.

"Brother William, I am glad to see you in the land of the living. Swallow this good draught and you will soon be as fit and strong as ever," she said cheerfully, helping him to sit up with one hand, and giving him the drink with the other.

It was then that Bradford realised that he had been carried into the very building that he had helped construct. He was lying in the makeshift hospital on the east side of the Common House, and there were a dozen other sick people nearby.

Outside, as Bradford could hear, his fellow Pilgrims were still hard at work.Considering their poor health, and inadequate diet, their achievements were little short of miraculous, but their conviction and determination seemed to carry them through every kind of obstacle. William Bradford recovered, but many of the Brethren did not survive the ordeals of sickness, hunger and cold in the harsh New England winter.

During the first three months of 1621, death became a common occurrence in the community. Two and sometimes three of them died every

The Mayflower *in Plymouth Harbour*

day, and it was as much as the others could do to bury their bodies. Of the hundred passengers who had sailed, fifty died in that first winter.

A few of the travellers had died at Cape Cod; for others, it seemed that the move to Plymouth was more than they could bear. Richard Britteridge was the first to die there, and he was soon followed by Christopher Martin, whose wife succumbed a few weeks later. This was very much the pattern. Husbands and wives often perished within days or weeks of each other. James Chilton, the oldest passenger, breathed his last in Cape Cod and was soon followed by his wife Susanna. At Plymouth, Francis and Sarah Eaton, Edward and Mary Fuller, William and Alice Mullens, John and Alice Rigsale, Edward and Agnes Tilley and Thomas and Jane Tinker all made the sad journey from the makeshift hospital to Burial Hill.

Captain Jones' crew fared little better. Alarmed by the speed with which the infection had spread through the community, the ship's Captain and his crew retreated to the *Mayflower*, but it soon became obvious that they had brought it with them, and many of them, too, fell ill and died. The graves of their companions were planted with corn, but they deliberately left the burial places unmarked so that the Indians would not know of the huge scale of their losses.

The extraordinary mental and physical strength of Miles Standish now began to show itself. He was not a Separatist, he had made that clear from the outset. He kept his beliefs to himself, but he regularly joined the Brethren at prayers on Sundays. When his wife had died he had grieved inwardly, but kept his pain to himself. All this while, he and the Brewsters had cared and tended the sick and dying. Often it was a gruelling and horrific job. At the same time, he continued to fulfil his responsibilities as their military leader. Small as he was, his strength seemed inexhaustible. He regularly conducted expeditions into the neighbouring countryside.

Ever since the Pilgrims had landed, they had seen smoke rising into the sky from the hills and woods around them. These grey plumed signals acted as a constant reminder that they were not alone. Some of the colonists found such signs of life more terrifying than the disease that was daily reducing their numbers. The weakest felt as though their lives lurched from one crisis to another, and their constant changes in fortune seemed more than they could bear. Their leaders took the opportunity of communal prayers to try to raise their lowered spirits.

One day in February, two Indians were seen on a nearby headland. Miles Standish had given orders that he should be informed immediately of any sighting of this kind. The little man bustled off with Stephen Hopkins in tow, and caught a glimpse of them on the horizon. He signalled that he wanted to open communications with them, but by the time they had reached the hilltop, the Indians had gone. Standish was in despair. He was convinced that the survival of the community depended on good relations with the Native Americans. He was not wrong.

Soon afterwards, he asked several of the Pilgrim leaders to meet him at the Common House. They sat on the rough-hewn benches, warmed by a meagre fire. Although it was still bitterly cold, they kept the fire low, for the roof thatch had nearly caught alight on several occasions.

"Gentlemen, you will have heard of our unsuccessful attempt to talk to the Indians today. It is imperative that I should be told of any contact they make. I must also inform you that yesterday the Indians came close enough to steal our tools when we were felling wood, yet we did not see them. They see us, but we do not see them. They do not wish to talk to us; they do not wish to know us. It is possible that we are in great danger, but I do not want the women to know of my fears . . . for they are already very afraid," he added, in a low voice.

"It seems to me that the natives are much less of a danger than the sickness that ravages us," said John Carver, who was now the Governor of the community.

Elder Brewster spoke, and, as usual, everyone listened. "We must be vigilant, but we must remember that we have not suffered at the hands of these people and may never do so. Vigilance and faith are our strongest allies, but if we submit unthinkingly to our fears, we may act unwisely."

"It may be that I can help you," said Christopher Jones, suddenly.

The Pilgrims turned to look at the Captain of the *Mayflower*, surprised to hear him speak, let alone come to their support. He had avoided them for the past two months, grudgingly letting them have some urgent supplies, but making his disapproval and irritation with them uncomfortably obvious.

"I could give you the means to protect yourselves, for the time being, at least. We could bring the cannons ashore and you could mount them. Thus you would be protected from the unknown dangers beyond."

This unexpected offer broke the deadlock between the Pilgrims and the *Mayflower*'s Captain, and marked a change in their strained relationship. The arrival of the big guns calmed the terrors of the vulnerable community. An impromptu party was held to celebrate the arrival of the artillery: Captain Jones brought a fat goose, the Pilgrims reciprocated with a crane and a mallard, and they feasted as cheerfully as they could, given the circumstances, confident of their new-found safety.

But they never needed the big guns.

"I am Samoset and I come in peace"

A month later, on a cold clear morning in mid March, an Indian strolled into the village. He was tall and tanned and clean-shaven. His shining black hair was cut short at the front, and long at the back. He wore a simple waist-band with a fringe, and carried a bow with two arrows, one without a head.

At the Common House, he was hailed by John Howland, now gaunt from lack of food and constant labouring, like all the men in the community. Howland challenged the solitary stranger.

"Stop, in the name of the Lord, and declare yourself," he said.

"I am Samoset, and I come in peace," was the reply, and the speaker smiled warmly.

"You speak English, then?" asked Howland, in utter amazement. He did. Minutes later the stranger was ushered into Elder Brewster's House, and was soon seated in the company of Miles Standish, Brewster himself, Bradford and John Carver.

So much was discovered that day. Samoset had learned a little English from the fishermen at Monhegan. He was a chief of the Pemaquids, and told the Pilgrims about the surrounding lands.

"You have neighbours," he said cheerfully. "They are the Pokanokets, men of the great Sachem Massasoit, and there are sixty of them. To the northeast another tribe, and these are Nausets. More of these. A hundred of them." They found out that it was the Nausets who had attacked them.

The men of the welcoming party were keen to be hospitable to their new friend. When it grew colder they put a riding coat over his shoulders, and plied him with drink and food – biscuits, butter, cheese, a piece of pudding and some cold duck. Even so, some of the Pilgrims did not trust him, and were frightened when Samoset didn't seem in any hurry to leave. They put him up in Stephen Hopkins's house, and before he left, they gave him a knife, a bracelet and a ring, which he received most graciously, promising to return with others and trade with them.

As good as his word, Samoset came back several days later with five tall young warriors. They were dressed in fringed deer skins, and their faces were painted, some with lines, others with stripes and some blackened from forehead to chin. They were tall, dark and poised, a striking contrast to the grey and sickly Pilgrims. They politely left their weapons outside the village and entered, intending to trade and negotiate, but it was Sunday, so the Pilgrims had to decline their offer. Nevertheless, the doors of communication had been opened, and relations with the Wampanoags began to grow from strength to strength, despite occasional misunderstandings.

On Thursday 22 March, a warm sunny day, Samoset arrived with a small group of compatriots. It was evident from their air of expectancy that there were important matters to be discussed, so Miles Standish, John Carver, William Brewster, William Bradford and Edward Winslow put aside their daily tasks, and sat down to talk to their visitors on some newly-hewn logs beneath a large oak tree.

"This is Tisquantum," said Samoset, adding "You can call him Squanto."

"I am delighted to make your acquaintance," said a tall, charismatic newcomer, and bowed gracefully to the company.

"We are delighted to meet you, sir. How did you learn to speak our language so fluently?" asked William Bradford.

"I was taken prisoner by Captain George Weymouth when I was just a boy. I was lured onto his ship. He intended to sell me as a slave, but by luck and good fortune I was taken to England, and then to London. There I lived in the house of Sir Ferdinando Gorges and worked for him as a translator on ships sailing to Virginia and along the American coast. Then I decided that I wanted to visit my people, for I had not seen them for many years, and I missed them. They lived here . . . in this place . . . in Patuxet. When I returned to look for my family and friends, they had all gone. They were dead, all dead, from the plague." He paused, staring ahead of him, as though he was trying to focus his mind on something else. There was a silence. Then William Brewster said,

"That must have been a great sadness for you."

"Yes . . . yes . . . It was," said Squanto, continuing in haste – "Then I worked for the Treasurer of the Newfoundland Company, Master John Slaney in the place you spoke of, which you call Cornhill. You may have seen our house there. Today we have come with gifts for you, which we have in the two baskets yonder." He strode off and returned with a beautiful leaf-wrapped parcel. It contained some fresh red herrings. Squanto then spoke to one of his fellow Wampanoags, who replied,

"Easu tommoc quocke. Occone."

"In the baskets you will find skins of beaver and also some good deerskins." The Pilgrims thanked them for their gifts.

At this point, the Wampanoags started to talk animatedly amongst themselves, and the Pilgrims asked Squanto to translate.

"There is an important matter we must explain, and we must not waste too much time about it. We have been sent by the great Sagamore Massasoit of the Pokanokets. He is yonder, on the hill, and you may see him

Squanto opened the way to peaceful negotiations

and his warriors there. They come in peace, and wish for your friendship."

This was exactly the message that Miles Standish had wanted to hear. The little group walked quickly up to the headland, and waited. Shortly afterwards, an extraordinary vision met their eyes: sixty Pokanokets lined up on the hill opposite them – an imposing but also an intimidating sight. Squanto proceeded to explain that the Sagamore Massasoit was there with his men because he wanted to meet the Pilgrim's leader alone, but this request was not greeted with any great enthusiasm. There was a momentary lull in the conversation, and suddenly Edward Winslow said,

"May I make a suggestion, Captain Standish? We must make a reciprocal gesture to the great Sachem. I will go as a representative of our people, and speak to him of peace, or even remain as hostage if he should choose to come to us . . . so long as this is acceptable to Governor Carver and Elder Brewster, of course." A brief debate followed, and his offer was accepted. Full of fear and expectation, and weighed down by a rucksack full of gifts, Edward Winslow set off to meet the Sagamore Massasoit, with Squanto by his side.

What the Pilgrims did not know was that Massasoit had seen more than half his people die in three terrible epidemics, and had subsequently been forced to submit to the rival Narragansett tribe. The Narragansetts lived in remoter places and so had less contact with Europeans and had not experienced the same sort of decline in population. With much greater numbers, the Narragansetts had exploited their position of strength over the Pokanokets. Massasoit was thus in need of support, and having watched the community of Pilgrims, with their women and children, and their efforts to build, plant and cultivate, had decided that they were not likely to be dangerous, yet they did have firearms, and might welcome an agreement with the Pokanokets. He was, of course, right.

After a mutual exchange of hostages and gifts, the two sides met in one of the newly constructed houses in the village. Sitting on a green rug with many cushions, having consumed a hearty meal, Massasoit, his supporters and the Pilgrims concluded the following pact:

1. That neither he nor any of his should injure or do hurt to any of our people.

2. And if any of his did hurt to any of ours, he should send the offender, that we might punish him.

3. That if any of our tools were taken away when our people are at work, he should cause them to be restored, and if ours did any harm to any of his, we would do the likewise to them.

4. If any did unjustly war against him, we would aid him; if any did war against us, he should aid us.

5. He should send to his neighbour confederates, to certify them of this, that they might not wrong us, but might be likewise comprised in the conditions of peace.

6. That when their men came to us, they should leave their bows and arrows behind them, as we should do our pieces when we came to them.

Lastly, that doing thus, King James would esteem of him as his friend and ally.

It was signed by Massasoit for the Pokanokets and Governor John Carver for the Pilgrims and Plymouth community. When the negotiations were over, the two leaders went to the brook, and embraced. Celebrations continued, for both sides were delighted to have concluded this peaceful agreement so painlessly and pleasantly. The next day a further meeting took place between Standish and Massasoit and his brother, Quadequina, which confirmed their friendship.

And then quite suddenly, the leader of the Pokanokets disappeared with all his men. He went almost as abruptly as he had arrived, leaving Squanto in the company of the Plymouth community, a man who was destined to contribute more to that community than any Pilgrim could have possibly ever imagined.

Chapter

14 THANKSGIVING

One sunny day in April, William and Mary Brewster and their young sons, Love and Wrestling, walked hand-in-hand down to the harbour. They were going to say goodbye to the *Mayflower* as she set out on her return journey to England.

"Will the *Mayflower* ever come back to us, mama?" asked ten-year-old Love. "She may. Perhaps she will bring your brother Jonathan and your sisters Patience and Fear when she returns," replied Mary.

"But are we not all alone now, papa, like orphans?" asked seven-year-old Wrestling. "No, my dear, we are never alone. God is always with us . . . and remember how many new friends we have found – all the Pokanoket people, and Squanto, who showed you how to play the pebble game, and who teaches us how to hunt and catch fish. God loves us and will help us to forge new friendships in our new home," explained Elder Brewster gently.

They looked out to the *Mayflower*, as she prepared to set sail. The voice of Captain Jones, giving orders to his crew could be heard in the distance, carried on the wind, faintly audible over the sound of the waves and the cries of the sea birds. The sails were unfurled and the anchor was raised. Finally she turned and, as the wind caught her sails, the little crowd on the waterside started to wave and wave and wave.

"Farewell!"

"Godspeed!"

'They looked out to the Mayflower *as she prepared to set sail'*

"God be with you!"

"Goodbye! Goodbye!"

Captain Jones and several of the men on deck waved back.

William Brewster turned to his wife, who brushed away a tear with the back of her hand.

Spring arrived, bringing new hope. They welcomed it and worked resolutely for the Merchant Adventurers who had invested in them, for their families and for God. The work was hard and unrewarding but there was more fresh food to eat, and every day it grew warmer. By April the numbers affected by the mysterious disease were falling, but now they suffered a new blow. Their Governor, John Carver, had some kind of seizure while he was working in the fields. Gripped by a terrible headache, he collapsed and died a few days later, much mourned and bitterly missed.

At Burial Hill, a small group stood under a clear blue spring sky. Birds were singing and a gentle warm breeze blew from the south. The body of John Carver was carefully lowered into the ground. The mourners at the graveside included William Bradford, William and Mary Brewster and Squanto. For Katherine Carver, the shock was too much, and she died, only five weeks later. Now she stood, pale and weak, leaning on the arm of young Desire Minter. Elder Brewster had chosen his text carefully:

"Brother John was our Governor. He was our champion and our supporter. He cared for us, as though we were his children. The words of John the Apostle speak to us today with words of love, just as our own Brother John spoke to us:

My children, let us not love in word, neither in tongue only, but in deed and in truth.

For thereby we know that we are of the truth and shall before Him assure our hearts.

For if our heart condemn us, God is greater than our heart, and knoweth all things.

Beloved, if our heart condemn us not, then have we boldness toward God. And whatsoever we ask, we receive of Him, because we keep His commandments, and do those things which are pleasing in His sight.

This is then His commandment, that we believe in the Name of His Son Jesus Christ, and love one another, as He gave commandment.

For he that keepeth His commandment dwelleth in Him, and He in him: and hereby we know that He abideth in us, even by the Spirit which He hath given us."

After Elder Brewster had said a prayer, four men with muskets fired three volleys, and the community stood in silence for three minutes, their heads bowed.

Now the Planters had to live up to their name, and they set to work to cultivate the fields. As it turned out, the quality of the soil was not as good as they had hoped, but because Squanto had lived there and knew the place, he explained to them the possibilities and limitations of the land. He gave them the greatest gift of all – his knowledge and experience. He taught the Planters which were the best crops to sow and explained that because the topsoil was poor, they would have to fertilise the ground; he showed them how to do this with fish meal. He taught them where to find the best shellfish in the harbour and where to fish for cod and bass. He often turned up with eel and game for them, and he taught them where to hunt, so that they had more and healthier food to eat.

In a few months Squanto had built a strong friendship with William Bradford, who realised how invaluable he was to the community – so much so that he thought of his Patuxet friend as a gift from God.

The *Mayflower*'s return was made with the prevailing west wind behind her, and only took 31 days, but she arrived many months after she had been expected, and the Merchant Adventurers, particularly Thomas Weston, were utterly disgusted that she had returned without a cargo. Later that year, news of Weston's anger and impatience reached William Bradford, the new Governor of the community.

The following summer months brought many new friendships and adventures with the neighbouring Indians. One new arrival at Plymouth was Hobbamock, a Wampanoag who moved into the community in July, and, like Squanto, made many important contributions. Meanwhile, Edward Winslow, Stephen Hopkins and Squanto had been to see Massasoit to discuss trading opportunities, a visit that confirmed their friendship with the Sachem. The following month the Nausets, the people who had attacked the Pilgrims the previous December, rescued and returned John Billington the younger to the colony, after he had got thoroughly lost in the woods and nearly died of exposure

Encouraged by the friendship and confidence of the colonists, the Sachem Massasoit decided that the time was right to reassert himself over his old rivals, and he attacked the Narragansetts. His success led to a moment of uncertainty for the Pilgrims, when it looked as if their peaceful relations with the Indians might be interrupted, but the Narragansetts came to an agreement with them, and all was well.

Autumn was marked by two memorable yet very different events, the bonding of the Pilgrims with the Pokanokets at the harvest Thanksgiving celebrations, and after that, the arrival of the sailing ship *Fortune*, which in several ways turned out rather less than fortunate.

The first Thanksgiving holiday was an impromptu happening that brought joy and merriment to all concerned. For the Pilgrims it was the moment when they gave thanks to God for His harvest gift and the care and love He had bestowed on them. For the Wampanoags it was the moment when they honoured the spirits of the sun and moon, the plants, crops, animals, air, earth, fire, wind and water for giving life and the seasonal wealth that they enjoyed. In that moment of similarity and difference, the two communities celebrated together.

The festivities had just begun. The Pilgrims were seated at a long table made of rough hewn planks that ran the length of the Common House. It was evening, and the days were now shorter. The happy faces of the company were lit by candlelight and they sat laughing and talking, with their trenchers full and a mug of beer before each and every one of them. In the middle of the table was a great plate piled high with every manner of fish and shellfish and another with turkey, goose and many kinds of fowl, large and small. The Pokanokets had also brought some fine venison to the feast.

"I fear that our present poverty prevents us from repaying you adequately for all the help and kindness you have shown us," said Governor

The First Thanksgiving

After gathering in a plentiful harvest to tide them over the next long winter, the Pilgrims dedicated to Providence a day of public Thanksgiving.

Bradford to Squanto, adding:

"Your talents have been essential to our success. The debt we owe you is beyond measure."

"It is your appreciation and your heart that are generous, Governor Bradford. As for my heart, I believe I have I found a small place there to fill the sadness and emptiness of the past. I feel as if Elder Brewster and Mistress Mary, Love and Wrestling, and you especially are now my family."

A little further down the table from Bradford, Miles Standish was seated between Massasoit and his brother Quadequina. Samoset sat at his right hand, busy translating what appeared to be a very animated conversation.

Squanto turned to Mary Brewster on his left and said,

"Governor Bradford is flattering me by saying I have many talents. If this is so, Mistress Brewster, which have you found most valuable today?" Mary Brewster laughed, and replied " Of course, first and foremost, keeping Love and Wrestling amused when they were quarrelling — this was the most valuable, and secondly, teaching me how to cook a turkey, something I would never have known before I came to this country."

"For my part," said Miles Standish, picking up the conversation, "It is the skill Squanto has taught us of how to catch a turkey, a secret every man should know who crosses the Atlantic in a sailing ship."

But William Bradford chipped in "Oh please, no. I have been made to feel very foolish trying to do this. I ended up face down in the mud when I tried it, and I believe the turkey still lives. I am so glad that this is not a skill that qualifies a man to be Governor." The company laughed loudly, particularly Massasoit and Quadequina, when they had been told what he had said. William Bradford felt happier than he had done for a long time.

Later that night, the women brought in great bowls of fruit, a colourful mix of seasonal and dried foods – strawberries, grapes, blueberries and plums. Everyone feasted well that night.

Earlier in the day, the Sachem Massasoit had arrived with ninety men. They were too many to seat in the Common House, but he and

Governor Bradford had decided that the feasting and merrymaking would continue for a further two days, both inside and outside the Common House, so that everyone – men, women and children – could join in the celebrations.

There was music and dancing. Both Roger Wilder and Richard Warren took out their whistles, and the Pokanokets had drums. They played hornpipes and jigs and many merry melodies and both the colonists and the Pokanokets danced their traditional dances, to each others' amusement, and sometimes amazement. There was so much laughter on all sides that for a few days, at least, the many differences in their ways of life seemed of little or no consequence.

The *Mayflower* never returned, but in November another sailing ship, the *Fortune*, arrived, bringing some thirty-five passengers. It was greeted with joy, for among those on board were Elder Brewster's son Jonathan, Edward Winslow's brother John, and Robert Cushman. But the ship had brought no supplies with it, and as the days and weeks unfolded, it became clear that the colony could scarcely support the extra mouths to feed. Now the festivities to celebrate the harvest seemed no more than a distant memory.

The *Fortune* sailed for England on December 13, 1621, taking with it Robert Cushman, who was under instructions from Thomas Weston to report back. Weston had sent the Pilgrims an unpleasant letter, saying that he had heard all about their troubles, but thought they only revealed their feebleness and lack of resolution. It was Governor Bradford's task to explain to the investors the problems they had encountered during that first winter, but his heart-rending letter failed to persuade Weston, and the problem of the debts owed by the Planters to the Merchant Adventurers was destined to grind on for many years to come.

The cargo that the *Fortune* took back to the old world represented the first fruits of the Planters, and was sent in partial repayment of their debts. It included many animal skins, such as beaver and otter, and also a great deal of timber, as much as could be loaded onto the vessel. Most valuable of all, perhaps, was the diary kept by William Bradford, which logged what had happened to the community on a day-to-day basis. It was intended for Pastor Robinson in Leiden, so that he at least would know the truth of what had befallen them. But as the *Fortune* drew near the English coast, she was seized by the French and held, and her whole cargo was taken. Everything was lost. The Pilgrims had been robbed of all their efforts.

By the end of May 1622, the situation had changed again. Other English visitors had arrived unexpectedly, including a sizeable number of men from another colony that Weston claimed he was setting up – all had to be fed. Their arrival exhausted their diminishing resources. The shortage of food was becoming a chronic problem.

Squanto, whose influence had increased far beyond his own expectations, now started to take advantage of his position of power. Treated with respect and even deference by the Pilgrims, he began to throw his weight around among the Wampanoags. If they did not agree to his wishes, he said he would release the white man's plague on them. His demands and expectations got out of hand, and eventually the Sachem Massasoit insisted to Governor Bradford that he was returned for execution.

The Pilgrims realised that they had to grant Massasoit's request, but tried to stall, and resorted to various excuses in an attempt to delay his return. Meanwhile, Squanto himself fell ill. He had been bleeding from the nose, a symptom that the Indians always regarded as fatal.

William Bradford arranged for him to be taken to the hospital within the Common House, and there he lay, slipping in and out of consciousness. On the last day of his life, Bradford sat at his friend's side. Now transformed by his illness, Squanto turned and whispered to him, "I shall soon die, I know it. Pray for me, Governor Bradford, that I may go to the Englishman's God in heaven." He paused and fell back onto the straw mattress. Shortly after that, he recovered consciousness again, and proceeded to bequeath his few possessions to the various friends he had made in the Pilgrim community, and whom he had grown to love. He died, soon afterwards. Remembering him many years later, Governor Bradford wrote,

"With some aberrations, his conduct was generally irreproachable, and his useful services to the infant settlement entitle him to grateful remembrance."

The Plymouth community continued to trade and negotiate with the various Wampanoag tribes, and Hobbamock began to take Squanto's place as their translator and negotiator. In March 1623, when Edward Winslow and Hobbamock were visiting the Pokanokets, Winslow won the love and respect of the Sachem Massasoit by successfully curing him of a serious illness. In gratitude to Winslow and the Pilgrim Fathers, Massasoit warned Hobbamock of a plot brewing against the English colony, and identified the perpetrators. With this information, Miles Standish was able to gather a small band of soldiers and deal quickly and effectively with the conspiracy.

In the spring of 1623, the Pilgrims re-organised their working arrangements. Now each family was given an area of land that was their own, and an acre was granted for each person. Families went to work with tremendous enthusiasm, and women and children joined in the efforts to plant corn. But now they faced a new difficulty; they had already planted all the seed-corn they had, and their stores of food were completely run down. Every day was uncertain; they did not know where their next meal would come from. They fished in relays, by day and night, they dug for shellfish in the sands, and sent out hunting parties to scour the surrounding countryside.

Towards the end of May the weather suddenly grew hot and dry, and by mid-June they were faced with drought and possible famine. When they went into the fields in July, they saw that their crops were turning brown, and beginning to ripen too early. They turned in their despair to their Elder, William Brewster. He advised them to set aside a day for prayer and fasting, when they would forget all their physical and material worries, and join together to ask God's help in their hour of need.

Under a glaring summer sun and a cloudless blue sky, a tired, hungry, group of men, women and children snaked its way from the little village into the fields beyond. They walked in silence in single file, with their heads bowed. At the front of that long line was Elder Brewster, wearing a large straw hat, a white linen shirt and his old leather breeches. When he came to a point mid-way between two fields, he stopped so that everyone could position themselves around him.

He opened the great Geneva Bible he had been carrying, and held it in the crook of his arm. He had chosen to start their prayers with the twenty-third Psalm. Of course, he had no need of the Bible because he knew the songs of David by heart, and so he was able to look into their eyes, and help them feel the beautiful old words of hope and faith:

> *The Lord is my shepherd, I shall not want.*
>
> *He maketh me to rest in green pastures, and leadeth me by still waters.*
>
> *He restoreth my soul and leadeth me in the paths of righteousness for His Name's sake.*
>
> *Yea though I should walk through the valley of the shadow of death, I will fear no evil: for thou art with me: thy rod and thy staff, they comfort me.*
>
> *Thou dost prepare a table before me in the sight of mine adversaries: thou dost anoint mine head with oil, and my cup runneth over.*
>
> *Doubtless kindness, and mercy shall follow me all the days of my life, and I shall remain a long season in the house of the Lord.*

They prayed with all their hearts, asking for God's help and love, so that the community would survive and continue to celebrate His goodness to them. Many hours later, they turned and left the fields to return to their house of prayer in the village. As Elder Brewster looked up, he saw dark clouds massing on the horizon for the first time in many weeks.

Their prayers had been answered. The rain had come.

15 THE TINDER BOX AND THE FLAME

July and August of 1623 marked a dramatic turning point in the fortunes of the Plymouth colonists, for even though they were destined to encounter many further trials, they would never face starvation again.

During those warm summer days, two ships sailed into Plymouth harbour – the *Anne* and the *Little James*. They brought mixed blessings. Many of the Leiden community who had been deeply missed were reunited with their friends and family at last. Among the newcomers were the two Brewster girls, Fear and Patience, as well as the wife of Samuel Fuller and Barbara, a young woman from Leiden, soon to marry Miles Standish. Another new arrival was a pleasant young widow from Somerset with two small sons. Her name was Alice Carpenter Southworth and she and Governor William Bradford were betrothed and married that same summer.

But not all the new arrivals fitted in so easily or liked what they found of the new life in the New World. For many of the second wave of Separatists from Leiden, their loved ones seemed to have changed almost beyond recognition: those that had crossed on the *Mayflower* two years earlier had been transformed by starvation, disease and the gruelling work regime they had undergone. They were now careworn, emaciated versions of their former selves. Their clothes were drab, weather-stained, patched and tattered. The simple log houses they had worked so hard to build were crude and uncomfortable in comparison to the graceful buildings and the well

Plymouth in 1622

laid-out cities that they had left behind. Worse still, the food was dreary and monotonous. Not all the tears shed on their arrival at Plymouth were tears of joy.

Governor Bradford quickly identified those travellers who would never settle down happily, or be able to accept the exacting routines of life in the new colony. He asked a number of them to return to England, and even paid for their passage.

The sheer demands of that busy life-style obliged the new arrivals to join in. As soon as they were they caught up in the business of working and living in that rapidly growing community, their frustrations and disappointments disappeared.

The following year another ship, the *Charity*, arrived, bringing cattle on board, and this in turn wrought another large change in their lives, diet and farming practices. The *Charity* also brought a clergyman, sent out by the Merchant Adventurers and the English government, who had become increasingly resentful of the Pilgrims' success, their Separatist faith, and their growing reputation on both sides of the Atlantic. The clergyman's task was to suppress their beliefs and bring them back to the

Anglican faith, to rule by bishops and archbishops. Needless to say, his attempts ended in failure.

Meanwhile, the relationship between the Planters and the Merchant Adventurers had not improved, so in the summer of 1625 Miles Standish returned to England, armed with letters explaining the business problems that confronted the community. Standish returned with all sorts of news, most of it bad. King James had died and been replaced by Charles I, who was said to have even less sympathy for non-conformists than his father, while Prince Maurice of Holland had also died. Robert Cushman, who had played such a key role in setting up the venture, was dead and worse still, many of their Separatist friends and relatives, both in England and Holland, had fallen victim to an outbreak of the plague.

One of the saddest pieces of news was of the death in Leiden of Pastor Robinson, a man whose unswerving faith in God had supported the community in England, Holland and even in the New World, where time and again his letters had uplifted their spirits. He was also greatly mourned by religious leaders and theologians at the University of Leiden, who had held him in high esteem. As for the Separatist community in Holland, his death was a blow from which it never really recovered. Their numbers dwindled away, and those that had not set sail for the New World were gradually assimilated into the Dutch population.

Despite his best efforts, Miles Standish failed to resolve the settlers' disagreements with the Adventurers, and these continued for another twenty-three years, until their debts were paid off in full.

But in other ways progress was being made, even if it was slow. By 1628, the colonists had created an orderly, well-kept neighbourhood with clean streets and thatched wooden houses in neat rows. Every home had its own garden patch, bright with flowers and vegetables and greatly loved and cared for, and each plot was neatly fenced. It was a model community. By 1630 the population of Plymouth had grown to three hundred.

And by then, change was in the air and people were either settling down or moving on. Taking his wife and children, Miles Standish left

Elder Brewster Preaching

Plymouth to set up home at Duxbury, Massachusetts. And other townships were being established nearby – Scituate, Taunton, Marshfield, Sandwich, Yarmouth, Barnstable, Seekonk and Nauset.

William Brewster continued to serve as Church Elder to the Plymouth community as well as teaching, tending his garden and working in the fields. He had aged considerably since the death of his wife Mary in 1625, but he worked almost continuously until his own death at the great age of seventy-nine.

Edward Winslow was adventurous by nature, and remained so. He had a passionate zest for life. He loved the Wampanoags as much as he loved the Pilgrim community and life on the move, and he regularly sailed between the Old World and the New. For a while, Winslow and Bradford shared the task of

Edward Winslow

Governor and during that time they grew increasingly close. Whenever Winslow went abroad, as he often did, William Bradford greatly missed his support and good humour. Both of them were historians and recorders by nature. They often wrote together, just as they worked together. Without their vivid accounts of the community, its trials and tribulations, we would know little or nothing of the *Mayflower* and her passengers, and this story could never have been written.

In 1654, on an extended visit to England, Edward Winslow was invited to work for Oliver Cromwell, by then Lord Protector of England, and ruling the country with his fellow Puritans. Winslow was given the title of Commissioner and sent off to recover the island of Hispaniola from the Spaniards, but after an abortive military expedition, he died at sea of a fever, on a voyage between Hispaniola and Jamaica. By then, he was sixty-five.

Governor Bradford's House in 1621

So William Bradford was left as Governor of the Plymouth community. Between 1628 and 1640, there was a massive exodus of Puritans from the Old to the New World, and with the rise of Puritanism in England, William Bradford and the Pilgrim Fathers became popular heroes, inspiring young and old alike.

One autumn day in 1637, Bradford was working at his desk. The setting sun was blazing through the window. The Governor's House was one of the largest in that little township, enjoying the best position and the special privilege of having windows made of glass. It also had a particularly fine garden and a number of cosy rooms with rugs and handsome furniture. It had served as the Bradfords' family home for a number of years. William and Alice had three children, William, Joseph and Mercy, and they had been joined by John Bradford, Dorothy's son from Leiden. He lived with his father and stepmother for a good while before moving on to Duxbury.

That afternoon there was a knock on the door and the young maidservant peered anxiously into the room to see if the Governor was busy. "Yes, Lizzy," he bellowed from his desk, for by now he was somewhat deaf. "What is it you want?"

"Please, sir, there is a Mr Simon Cooper at the door. He says he has business with you, on account of his father in England."

"Show him in, Lizzy, show him in."

A tall gangly youth dressed in brown breeches and a linen shirt came into the room, carrying a large wooden box. Governor Bradford invited him to pull up a stool and explain his purpose. The young visitor immediately started to chatter nervously.

"Please, your honour, I have come from my father in Boston, although I'd like to settle here myself, which is why I am here with my family. I am a carpenter, sir, and that is what I do, only that is not why I am here, sir, for I am here to give you this box which is a gift from my father who knew you in Boston, sir, and that is why I am here, if you understand my meaning, sir."

"In Boston? I cannot recall any friends or acquaintances from Boston."

"Please, your honour, my father says that you were a prisoner entrusted to his care, when you were both young, younger than I am now, and it was his duty to guard you, but he played games with you instead. And he never forgot you, and he always said that you had opened his heart to God, for all you were so young, which is why he has sent you this box, sir, if you take my meaning."

"Show me, brother Simon," said Governor Bradford, a little wearily, for he had been hard at work since five that morning. Simon Cooper carried the wooden box over to the Governor and laid it at his feet. Bradford lifted the lid. Inside was a leather-bound Bible, a set of knucklebones and a letter. Bradford carefully took out the letter, broke the seal, and read it:

To my esteemed friend and brother in the Lord, William Bradford, Governor of Plymouth Plantation, Greetings.

Thirty years ago, you and Pastor Clifton, Mr Robinson and Mr Brewster were all prisoners in the Guildhall prison at Boston. I was then scarcely more than a boy, but it fell to my lot to guard you and we became acquainted, and played the game of knucklebones.

Although I guarded you carefully, and took my duties seriously, I never needed to worry that you would try to escape, for you were all honourable men of God, and the most honest and kind men that were ever to suffer in that prison. Your bravery and faith in the Lord touched the hearts of many in Boston, myself included, and so today our city is known to be God-fearing, and to support the true faith, and will always do so, however we may suffer for it.

Now, Sir, you are a famous man, and all that know you say that you are just and true, as I know full well, so I am sending you this Bible, as a gift, with my son, who is a carpenter and will soon, God willing, be working in the land you have made your blessed home. He comes with his wife and son.

Please welcome him to your town of Plymouth for he is a virtuous and upright young man, and the apple of my eye, just as you were for Master Brewster, who loved you as his own son.

May God bless you, Mr Bradford, and all your family, for we of Boston will never forget you. You have lit a fire in our hearts and we will always remember you.

Your servant,

John Cooper

July 30 anno 1637

The Pilgrims left England to live their lives and practise their faith as they wanted. They established a system of order and democracy before they even landed on the rock by getting all the men on the *Mayflower* to sign the Compact. Once in the New World, they maintained their religious independence, keeping a certain distance between themselves and the old homeland, for they believed that a community should act together, and all should have a voice in its decisions.

More than a hundred years after the death of William Bradford in 1655, North America once again asserted its independence of England, her bishops and her king. After the Revolution, the Declaration of Independence of 1776 proclaimed thirteen colonies free from English rule, and set the stage for the creation of the world's greatest republic. The United States' Constitution aimed to put the Pilgrims' ideal of democracy into practise.

The tiny flame that fired this great national movement towards independence and responsible federal government was lit from the tinder box of a frail but heroic band of families, the first families that ever set off for America's shores. In the autumn of 1620 one hundred and two people set sail from England in a ship no more than ninety feet long and twenty-six feet wide.

Signing the Declaration of Independence

Interest in the Pilgrim Fathers took off in America during the nineteenth century. By that time, the country was poised to become one of the richest and most powerful countries in the world. William Bradford's precious manuscript containing the History of Plymouth Plantation had been stolen by the British during the Revolution, but it turned up again,

unexpectedly and most wonderfully, in 1854. America was ready to take a new pride in her own history, and the bravery and determination of the earliest pioneers. Poems and stories were written about them and their leaders, and this thrilling yet alarming episode in American history was often retold.

Abraham Lincoln

The reconstruction of the Mayflower

In 1863, Abraham Lincoln, inspired by the Pilgrims' report of their first harvest Thanksgiving, decided to establish it as a national holiday. At first, it was celebrated on the last Thursday in November, but in 1939 it was redefined as the fourth Thursday in November, although the Pilgrim Fathers had probably celebrated their harvest Thanksgiving some time in October.

If you visit Plymouth today, you can see the rock on which the Pilgrims first landed, and go on board a model of the *Mayflower*, with its narrow decks and small wooden berths, and hear how the sailors would have talked in 1620. You can also visit a historical reconstruction of the Plantation itself which shows you how the Pilgrims lived from day to day, and you can see what they saw when they looked out to sea, across that wide, beautiful bay. But it was their hearts, minds and imaginations that changed the world. Let us revisit them for the last time, at a moment when these were most fully engaged.

It is a Sunday evening in spring, and the Scrooby Separatists are gathered in their simple wooden church as Elder Brewster leads them into the 86th Psalm. He has chosen it specially, knowing how well it expresses the sufferings they have endured, and they are singing with all their hearts, finding their own feelings reflected in it. We can pick out the booming voice of William Bradford, who stands between Alice and his stepson John. The light tenor voice of Edward Winslow can also be heard. Somewhere a few rows back a baby is wailing softly – she wants her supper now. The words they sing, like their vision, transcends time:

> *Incline thine ear, Oh Lord, and hear me: for I am poor and needy.*
>
> *Preserve thou my soul, for I am merciful; my God, save thou thy servant, that trusteth in thee.*
>
> *Be merciful unto me, oh Lord, for I cry upon thee continually.*
>
> *Rejoice the soul of thy servant: for unto thee, Oh Lord, do I lift up my soul . . .*
>
> *In the day of my trouble I will call upon thee: for thou hearest me . . .*
>
> *For great is thy mercy toward me, and thou hast delivered my soul from the lowest grave.*
>
> *Oh God, the proud are risen against me, and the assemblies of violent men have sought my soul, and have not set thee before them.*
>
> *But thou, Oh Lord, art a pitiful God and merciful, slow to anger and great in kindness and truth.*
>
> *Turn unto me, and have mercy upon me: give thy strength unto thy servant, and save the son of thine handmaid.*
>
> *Show a token of thy goodness towards me, that they which hate may see it, and be ashamed, because thou, Oh Lord, hast helpen me and comforted me.*
>
> *Amen.*

BIBLIOGRAPHY

Primary Sources

Bradford, William, *Of Plymouth Plantation: Bradford's History of Plymouth Plantation, 1606-1646*. William Davis, ed. (Barnes & Noble, 1964)

Bradford, Winslow et al., *Chronicles of the Pilgrim Fathers of the Colony of Plymouth, 1602-1625*. Alexander Young, ed. (Da Capo Press, 1971)

The Geneva Bible: A facsimile of the 1560 edition
(University of Wisconsin Press, 1969)

Secondary Sources

Adair, John, *Puritans, Religion and Politics in 17th Century England and America* (Sutton Publishing, 1998)

Ashton, Robert, *Reformation and Revolution* (Paladin Books, 1985)

Brogan, Hugh, *The Penguin History of the USA* (Penguin Books, 2001)

Brown, John, *The Pilgrim Fathers of New England and their Puritan Successors* (The Religious Tract Society, 1897)

Cockshott, Winnifred, *The Pilgrim Fathers: Their Church and Colony* (Methuen, 1909)

Colloms, Brenda, *The Mayflower Pilgrims* (Wayland Publishers, 1973)

Copley Baines, R.S., *The Reluctant Adventurers* (New Choir Alley Press, 2000)

Gill, W.J.C., *The Pilgrim Fathers* (Longman, 1971)

Jessup, Edmund F., *The Mayflower Story* (Whartons, 1962)

Miller, Perry & Johnson, Thomas H., *The Puritans: A Sourcebook of their Writings* (Harper & Row, 1963)

Sears Nickerson, W., *Land Ho! 1620: A Seaman's Story of the Mayflower, her Construction, her Navigation, and her First Landfall.* Delores Bird Carpenter, ed., (Michigan State University Press, 1997)

Websites

Caleb Johnson's *Mayflower* Web Pages
http://www.members.aol.com/calebj/mayflower.html

The Pilgrim Archive
http://www.pilgrimarchives.nl/html/the pilgrimarchive/tpa_eng.html

Plimoth Plantation. The Living History Museum of 17th Century Plymouth
http://www.plimoth.org/Museum/museum.htm

Mayflower
http://www.pilgrims.net/plymouth/history/mayflower.html

The *Mayflower* Society
http://www.mayflower.org/history.htm